Appreciative Sharing of Knowledge

Leveraging Knowledge Management For Strategic Change

Tojo Thatchenkery

George Mason University

Taos Institute Publications
Chagrin Falls, Ohio, U.S.A.

APPRECIATIVE SHARING FOR KNOWLEDGE
Leveraging Knowledge Management for Strategic Change

Reprint 2011

FIRST EDITION

Taos Institute Publications
Chagrin Falls, Ohio, U.S.A.

ISBN: 978-0-7880-2137-4
LCN: 2004112439

PRINTED IN THE UNITED STATES OF AMERICA

Introduction To Taos Institute Publications

The Taos Institute is a nonprofit organization dedicated to the development of social constructionist theory and practices for purposes of world benefit. Constructionist theory and practice locate the source of meaning, value and action in communicative relations among people. Chief importance is placed on relational process and its outcomes for the welfare of all. Taos Institute Publications offers contributions to cutting-edge theory and practice in social construction. These books are designed for scholars, practitioners, students and the openly curious. The **Focus Book Series** provides brief introductions and overviews that illuminate theories, concepts and useful practices. The **Books for Professionals Series** provides in-depth works, which focus on recent developments in theory and practice. Books in both series are particularly relevant to social scientists and to practitioners concerned with individual, family, organizational, community and societal change.

Kenneth J. Gergen
President, Board of Directors
The Taos Institute

For information about the Taos Institute visit: www.taosinstitute.net

Taos Institute Publications

Focus Book Series

The Appreciative Organization, (2001) by Harlene Anderson, David Cooperrider, Kenneth J. Gergen, Mary Gergen, Sheila McNamee, and Diana Whitney

Appreciative Leaders: In the Eye of the Beholder, (2001) Edited by Marge Schiller, Bea Mah Holland, and Deanna Riley

Experience AI: A Practitioner's Guide to Integrating Appreciative Inquiry and Experiential Learning, (2001) by Miriam Ricketts and Jim Willis

Appreciative Sharing of Knowledge: Leveraging Knowledge Management for Strategic Change, (2005) by Tojo Thatchenkery

Social Construction: Entering the Dialogue, (2004) by Kenneth J. Gergen and Mary Gergen

Books for Professionals Series

SocioDynamic Counselling: A Practical Guide to Meaning Making, (2004) by R. Vance Peavy

Experiential Learning Exercises in Social Construction – A Fieldbook for Creating Change, (2004) by Robert Cottor, Alan Asher, Judith Levin, and Cindy Weiser

Dialogues About a New Psychology, (2004) by Jan Smedslund

For on-line ordering of books from Taos Institute Publications visit www.taosinstitute.net

For further information, write or call: 1-888-999-TAOS, 1-440-338-6733, info@taosinstitute.net or books@taosinstitute.net

Table Of Contents

Acknowledgments

In undertaking this endeavor, I have learned that writing a short Focus book can be harder than writing a long scholarly one. Fortunately, I received good help from and am indebted to several talented individuals. Carol Metzker helped immensely in reworking my academically oriented manuscript into one that would appeal to an audience more interested in practice and application. Kenneth Gergen offered valuable feedback to help me reframe the manuscript for the Taos Institute Focus Book series. Jane Seiling and Jackie Stavros, accomplished authors of related appreciative inquiry publications read the manuscript several times and offered very useful suggestions. They also played a key role as Taos Institute Senior Editors in helping me revise the manuscript according to the Focus Book guidelines.

The person who worked the most with me in bringing out this Focus Book is Jane Seiling. She believed in the ideas described in the book deeply and went the extra mile to help me stay focused in communicating the principles and practices of *appreciative sharing of knowledge*. Jane constantly offered suggestions and helped me see things from different perspectives. She was detail oriented but also saw the bigger picture.

The Vice-president, the managers, and the specialized staff at the financial services institution at which I applied the ASK method deserve special credit for their open mindedness and flexibility in trying out a new approach. Their commitment and enthusiasm for the ASK project narrated in this Focus Book made the experience a positive one for all involved.

I am grateful to Sue Hammond of Thin Book Publishing who suggested the idea of writing a short book for practitioners and helped significantly in an earlier version of the manuscript.

I also thank Dawn Dole, Harlene Anderson, and Mary Gergen of Taos Institute, David Runk of Fairway Press, and Peter Staffel for his editorial help. Last but not least, I am indebted to my wife Tessy and daughter Sruthi for their constant support.

To Tessy and Sruthi
in appreciation of their love and knowledge sharing.

Preface

How to manage knowledge effectively is a question that has run through the literature of the field of organizational behavior for many years. Knowledge has been examined from many angles: how it is created (creativity, scanning the environment), how it is shared (network analysis, communication patterns), and how it is applied (decision making, problem solving). What Tojo Thatchenkery has finally done in *Appreciative Sharing of Knowledge: Leveraging Knowledge Management for Strategic Change* is to help us understand a simple process for getting at what it takes to actually *improve* these processes in an organization. Although the "Appreciative Sharing of Knowledge" or "ASK" approach described here is focused primarily on the act of sharing knowledge, the methodology described in this simple but important book can be applied to a wide range of knowledge management challenges and opportunities.

Many organizations have recognized the need to improve knowledge sharing processes. People at Unilever, the consumer products giant, are fond of saying "If only Unilever knew what Unilever knew." In every large, complex organization, the amount of knowledge that is actually shared and applied to organizational opportunities is a tiny fraction of the total knowledge that exists among members of the firm. Of course, information technology and accessible databases have done a great deal to provide people with access to facts, documents and other types of routine, transactional knowledge. We might refer to this kind of knowledge as "know what." While "know what" knowledge is important, there is another kind of knowledge that is perhaps even more critical to organizations. We might call this kind of knowledge "know how."

"Know how" tends to be more emergent and more tacit. It is best shared not through databases, but via interactions among people that involve explanations, examples, or demonstrations. Until now, leaders have been without an effective process for doing anything practical or powerful about improving the amount of "know how" that is transferred among members of their enterprise.

The ASK method described by Thatchenkery provides a simple method for discovering and strengthening processes that *already exist* in an organization for sharing "know how." Because it is based on an Appreciative Inquiry (AI) approach, the ASK method doesn't involve the installation of complex IT systems or forcing people to exhibit new behaviors requiring training or special incentives. Instead, the ASK approach uncovers things that people in an organization already do to share knowledge with one another and then seeks to involve them in experimenting with ways to strengthen those naturally occurring processes.

Thatchenkery illustrates the application of the ASK method through a case study of a bank that is concerned with the amount of knowledge it is losing each day as people retire or leave the organization for various reasons. Leaders of the bank recognized that in order to compete, they couldn't let the knowledge its employees had accumulated leave the organization with them. They needed to find more effective ways to help people share knowledge while they were still employed. Thatchenkery explains that people in the bank were acquainted with techniques used for "retrospective" learning, like the Army's After Action Review process, in which events are dissected to determine the causes of problems, but that they found these methods unpopular with employees because they seemed more focused on placing blame than on learning. The bank preferred an approach that would allow people to share what Thatchenkery calls "prospective" knowledge, which is knowledge that they may need to be successful in the future. To do this, the leaders of the bank discovered that they needed to step aside and allow people to discover for themselves what worked, rather than mandating a knowledge sharing policy or procedure.

Readers looking for shortcuts need to understand that what is important is going through the process of discovering the unique practices that already exist and that are supported by the culture of each organization rather than installing an "off the shelf" knowledge sharing practice. Part of what makes the ASK methodology powerful is that people give the challenge of sharing knowledge more thought and in the process of doing so, become more committed to doing things that make it possible.

Sharing knowledge is a perfect target for the application of AI methods because sharing knowledge with others is a positive act. While there are those who are reluctant to share knowledge with others because they associate knowledge with power, the majority of people in organizations would readily share what they know with others if they could. In fact, most are hungry to do so. Hence, there is positive motivation to engage in a process like ASK that provides an opportunity for people to be recognized by others for what they can contribute.

Through the case, Thatchenkery demonstrates the steps that should be taken to apply the ASK methodology. While the chapters are short, easy reading, they still convey the importance of investing time and energy in executing the ASK approach. Like most other methods of changing organizational behavior, what you get back from ASK depends on what you put into it. The approach isn't hard to understand, and Thatchenkery makes it even easier to follow by ending each chapter in a Focus Box with notes for practitioners that reemphasize the critical points made. While some new language is introduced here (I personally love the idea of calling internal consultants in this process "knowledge ambassadors") the reader won't be put off by too much academic theory. Thatchenkery gives enough background to acknowledge the sources of some underlying premises but doesn't make it a chore for readers to grasp the essence of the ASK approach. Those interested in understanding more deeply concepts involving the social construction of knowledge or the building of social capital in organizations are referred to the appropriate authors.

I expect a lot from this Focus Book. The need it addresses is clear and for a change, so is the answer.

William Pasmore
Partner, Mercer Delta Consulting
New York.

Chapter 1

Introduction

Imagine an organization where you pick up your phone, call a co-worker from a different project in another division, state, or country to ask how she handled a challenging situation, and get an extremely useful response. This in turn stimulates a conversation that leads to brainstorming, solutions, and innovation. Plus, the cost to your division is only an offer of a thank you and the recognition of your co-worker: no lengthy, time-consuming research program, no unnecessary documenting of information. It is quick, painless, perhaps even fun, and people created instead of diminished relationships in the process. Change and learning occur through such relationships, creating opportunities for both the employees and the organization to grow while actively sharing knowledge.

Does it sound too good to be true? Not to Green Capital Bank,[1] a well-known financial institution that integrates an approach to knowledge management called *Appreciative Sharing of Knowledge* [ASK] to create a culture of true knowledge sharing that positively impacts the bottom line.

Knowledge management has emerged as one of the most active areas of research and practice for improving organizational efficiency and quality of life. Hundreds of consultants who had developed strong practices with re-engineering have redefined themselves as change agents directly addressing knowledge management issues that impair change in organizations. Organizations of all sorts, for-profit, nonprofit, and public sectors alike, have developed knowledge management strategies, processes, or practices, even if they don't recognize or acknowledge the changes they have made.

Terms like intellectual capital, knowledge industry, knowledge society, knowledge age, knowledge worker, knowledge creation, and knowledge sharing appear in all forms of business media. In addition, a new genre of professional titles for those responsible for knowledge management in organizations has emerged, such as chief knowledge officer, chief learning officer, and knowledge architect, adding credence to the need for knowledge generation and retention inside organizations. Occasionally, these efforts, as in Green Capital Bank, occur through the efforts of human resource, organizational development, or "learning" departments."

This *Focus Book* will tell the story of this organization and the efforts of its learning department to create strategic organizational change through knowledge management. Knowledge management was critical for maintaining the competitiveness of the Green Capital Bank in the banking industry. The organizational learning department recognized managing knowledge as the most effective way for creating strategic change in the Green Capital Bank. Aware of the fast pace of change in the financial services industry, they saw the need to be proactive and think innovatively.

Though there is no agreed upon definition of "knowledge management," the term generally refers to a broad spectrum of organizational practices, methods, processes, and approaches coalescing around the task of generating, capturing, and sharing the know-how, specialized knowledge, expertise, and best practices relevant to the core business of an organization. The following items are generally considered integral components of knowledge management:

- Generating new knowledge internally and accessing valuable knowledge from outside sources

- Representing knowledge in documents, databases, and software
- Facilitating knowledge growth through culture and incentives
- Transferring existing knowledge throughout the organization
- Creating awareness of the benefits of retaining knowledge within the organization as changes occur and people leave.

In summary, knowledge management has both technical and social aspects. The technical dimension has received most of the attention and resources leading to the development of hundreds of "KM Architectures," essentially knowledge management collaborative software. Recently, the latter social dimension has become more visible as the technical side has matured and practitioners beginning to appreciate the "soft" people management side of knowledge management.

Why Knowledge Management?

What is the basis for this increased attention for knowledge management? Part of the answer lies in the belief that we are living in a knowledge economy or knowledge society where the primary exchange code is information-turned-knowledge. Those who have it, or have more than others, have a competitive advantage. Hence, if organizations want to maximize chances for success, they must have a plan for the creation, sustenance, and sharing of knowledge.

Knowledge has always played an important role in societal advance. In 800 B.C., Indian mathematicians built upon generations of knowledge to develop mathematics that is quite sophisticated even by today's standards. Phoenicians were implicitly concerned with how knowledge about trade logistics and merchant practices was built, transferred to employees, and successfully applied. With such roots, claiming that we now live in a "knowledge society" as if it were unique is no more informative than saying that we now live in a "power society" or "money society" or "culture society."[2]

Knowledge management is rooted in many disciplines, including economics, education, information management, organizational behavior, psychology, and sociology. Knowledge management embraces the perspectives developed in these subject areas but operates from the basic premise of the tacit nature of knowledge. *Tacit knowledge* is personal knowledge rooted in individual experience and involving personal belief, perspective, and values. Philosopher of science Michael Polyani (1967) famously characterized tacit knowledge as that "which we know but cannot tell." A key aspect of knowledge management is finding ways to apprehend the tacit knowledge of long-time employees, customers, clients, or other stakeholders.

Making good use of tacit knowledge, however, is a challenging task. Typically, employees may not want to share what they know, fearing that once they share their specialized knowledge, they may not be needed. Therefore, encouraging those who have tacit knowledge to share it organization-wide is vital. This book attempts to respond to this situation in two ways: first, by introducing ASK, or appreciative sharing of knowledge; second, by encouraging the important but often unrecognized and underappreciated potential of knowledge management for initiating or facilitating organizational change. I suggest that knowledge management is inherently embedded in change, particularly in the dynamic quality of knowledge-as-a-sense-of-worth.

Knowledge is dynamically embedded in networks and processes as well as in the human beings who constitute and use them. In other words, people typically acquire knowledge from established organizational routines, the entirety of which are usually impossible for any one person to know. The acquiring of knowledge is, in essence, a mutually constructed activity. To build it alone and to keep it to oneself is to create a singleness of mind—taking away the usefulness of the knowledge, wisdom, and aspirations of the "knower(s)."

Philosopher of science and psychologist Kenneth Gergen (1999) suggests, "If we are to generate meaning together we must develop smooth and reiterative patterns of interchange—a dance in which we move harmoniously together" (p. 160). He suggests that to mutually construct our world, we must engage in a coordinating discourse with a significance of self-expression, active mutual affirmation, and regular recreation of our worlds (1999, pp.158-164). Within this conceptual framework Taos Institute bases its Focus Book, *Appreciative sharing of knowledge: Leveraging knowledge management for strategic change*. Appreciative sharing of knowledge [ASK] becomes an integral part of organizing—whether in the workplace or otherwise—when an invitation to bring together and share knowledge occurs. As the knowledge sharing gains momentum, the positive energy generated softens the *resistance to change* typically encountered in most change efforts and empowers individuals to positively impact organizational change. Throughout the book, this dual focus—initiating ASK and leveraging it for change—will be evident.

Turning Knowledge Management into Knowledge Sharing

In practice, knowledge management often encompasses identifying and mapping intellectual assets within the organization, generating new knowledge for competitive advantage within the organization, making vast amounts of corporate information accessible, and sharing practices and technology that enables all of the above, including groupware and intranets.

A common thread links collaborative learning and other recent business strategies: information and knowledge are vital corporate assets, so businesses need strategies, policies, and tools to manage these assets. Though this need to manage knowledge seems obvious, few businesses have acted on this understanding. Such actions typically range from technology-driven methods of accessing, controlling, and delivering information to massive efforts to change corporate culture.

Integrating Appreciative Philosophy and Social Constructionism with Knowledge Management

Combining the principles of Appreciative Inquiry (AI),[3] social constructionism,[4] and knowledge management, this book describes an approach called ASK—*Appreciative Sharing of Knowledge*. The goals of appreciative sharing of knowledge [ASK] are to identify the talents and competencies already at work in the organization, to locate what knowledge-sharing practices already exist, and to enhance the values and behaviors that enable knowledge sharing. The case study in the next chapter provides an example of such a knowledge-sharing paradigm and helps the reader learn more about locating and sustaining knowledge that matters in organizations, thereby opening up immediate and future organizational possibilities.

A brief review of the key principles of AI, social constructionism, and knowledge management (the core elements and structure of ASK) will aid in understanding the logic, rationale, and basic tenets of appreciative sharing of knowledge.

AI is an innovative action research model introduced in 1986 that has become popular with a large number of organization development practitioners worldwide. In a thought-provoking article written in 1987, David Cooperrider and Suresh Srivastva propose that by focusing on what is working in an organization as opposed to what is not working, one can learn more about the "life giving forces" of an organization and follow-up with action steps to enhance them. During the nearly two decades since its introduction, AI has become more mainstream and has been used in an increasing number of issues and settings.

The foundation of AI lies in the established school of social constructionism and hermeneutics, the German philosophical tradition of the study of interpretation, expounded by philosophers such as Habermas, Wittgenstein, Gadamer, and Ricoeur.[5] One of the distinguishing features of social constructionism is the linguistic turn that has prompted social scientists to recognize the force with which language shapes the course and meaning of human affairs. Social constructionists see language as the basic vehicle by which we construct the reality of our shared world. Sociologists Berger and Luckman's (1966) well-known treatise on the *social construction of reality* revolutionized the sociology of knowledge discourse.

Two decades later postmodern thinkers such as Foucault and Derrida have strengthened Berger and Luckman's view regarding language and discourse as the force through which humans create the historical and cultural traditions that in turn create a *self-referential*[6] (Lyotard, 1984; 1988) reality, that is, reality that derives its significance from the context and the interdependencies of the elements constituting it. Since then, well known social scientist Kenneth Gergen has adapted this way of thinking to the fields of Organization Science, Psychology, and the general discourses. He provides an extremely persuasive and accessible narrative of the linguistically constituted nature of social reality in *An Invitation to Social Construction* (1999).

Knowledge management—the third core element and structural support of ASK—is not about technology infrastructure or tools, though that is where most of the money has been spent so far, not surprisingly, since one of the distinguishing elements of modernity is over-reliance on tools. During the initial years of explosive growth of knowledge management, organizations worldwide invested heavily in knowledge management tools, adhering with the blind faith to the maxim "if you build, they will use it."

New Assumptions about Knowledge Sharing

During the last five years, most Chief Information Officers [CIOs] of large corporations have realized that knowledge management is not about managing but about sharing. A culture that encourages knowledge sharing first needs to exist for any knowledge management technology infrastructure to work. The question then is "How does one create a culture of sharing?" ASK answers that question.

The following case study shows how the ASK process creates a culture of knowledge sharing, thereby changing the thinking of key stakeholders. This, in turn, creates opportunities for an entire culture to change to or adopt a more relational form not previously recognized as possible. This *Focus Book* distills lessons learned from this and other applications into a step-by-step process that an interested practitioner can readily adapt to his or her unique circumstances and demands.

Seven-Steps to a Relationship-Based Process

Appreciative sharing of knowledge or ASK is a seven-step approach and will be explained in detail in the next several chapters. The purpose of ASK is to give employees and other stakeholders of an organization the opportunity together to set a course of action in building a corporate culture that values sharing what is known and important. Chapters 2 through 8 provide the narrative of Green Capital Bank's [GCB] experience in utilizing appreciative sharing of knowledge. The chapters provide a rich illustration of how the ASK process worked for the Green Capital Bank and describe practical "lessons learned" and "reflections" about knowledge sharing from this unique case study. Following the narrative example, the text shows how the Green Capital Bank's experiences can be applied to or adapted for other organizations' successful knowledge sharing processes and anticipates results for other organizations.

At the end of each chapter, a box labeled "Practitioner Focus Box" highlights the major steps of ASK, so that knowledge management practitioners, organizational development consultants, and other professionals can use the methodology for initiating their own knowledge sharing interventions.

Knowledge sharing is of crucial importance in societal evolution. The survival of humanity has been attributed to many things such as leadership, the prevailing of the good over the evil, and political ideologies (democracy over totalitarianism). In this book, Appreciative Sharing of Knowledge [ASK] is added as yet another process of change that has positively impacted the evolution of industrial society.

Chapter Summary

The key question this chapter considers is: How does one create a new knowledge sharing culture as quickly and painlessly as possible? To help answer this question, the text provides a review of the current status of knowledge management, the historical development of it, and the various factors responsible for its evolution. Various stages in the development of the field of knowledge management, such as the over-reliance on technology, prediction and control, and the later realization that knowledge management is not about "managing" but about "sharing," were also described. Knowledge management has been practiced since the onset of human civilization and therefore should not be considered a recent need or phenomenon arising only in the current high-technology society. Most importantly, historically successful knowledge-sharing cultures were appreciative in nature (Ehin, 2000).

Further, this chapter describes the creation of a model of knowledge management that would combine the principles of AI and knowledge sharing. The result is a new model of knowledge management called ASK, or *appreciative sharing of knowledge*. [The acronym ASK is used throughout this book though its expansion, appreciative sharing of knowledge is also mentioned several times to help the readers remember what ASK stands for]. The chapter also touches upon the latest postmodern intellectual discourses of social constructionism, hermeneutics, and AI that support the various tenets of ASK.

Practitioner Focus Box

Appreciative sharing of knowledge, or ASK, typically consists of seven steps. The following chapters in this book describe these steps in detail.

Seven Steps to ASK, or Appreciative Sharing of Knowledge

Step 1. Set the stage. Present the appreciative knowledge sharing paradigm and negotiate top management commitment and support.

Step 2. Through paired interviews, elicit positive stories of successful knowledge sharing behaviors already occurring.

Step 3. Identify knowledge enablers [KE].

Step 4. Analyze the data using knowledge infrastructure factors [KIF].

Step 5. Construct possibility propositions.

Step 6. Consensually validate and rank possibility propositions.

Step 7. Form an implementation team. Then execute!

Chapter 2

Initiating ASK, Appreciative Sharing of Knowledge

This chapter describes various antecedent factors in the initiation of the appreciative sharing of knowledge [ASK] process at the Green Capital Bank. The process began with something different than the ASK methodology. I was hired as a consultant to help the client system examine various knowledge management issues that they had been trying to deal with for several months. The antecedent factors narrated in this chapter include historical and contextual aspects. Learning about the Green Capital Bank example should enable readers to better appreciate the importance of developing a reasonable working knowledge of the antecedent factors before deciding on a methodology.

Knowledge Sharing in Green Capital Bank

The Green Capital Bank [GCB] is one of United States' largest diversified financial services organizations, providing regional banking, corporate banking, real estate financing, asset-based lending, asset management, global fund services, and mortgage banking. In the late 1990s, after a series of mergers and acquisitions, knowledge sharing at Green Capital Bank was declining. When departing employees lost their jobs due to redundancy, they took vast amounts of important knowledge with them. Moving into a defensive mode, many of the remaining employees kept their local knowledge to themselves for competitive advantage over their co-workers.

In order to re-establish a climate for the knowledge sharing that would see the bank through the many changes in industry policy, processes, and technology, the bank's organizational learning department began to study the latest thinking on knowledge management as a way to re-incorporate knowledge sharing in Green Capital Bank. This department was responsible for the training and professional development of all company employees. Their goal was to keep management and employees across business units up-to-date with current best practices, processes, technology, laws, and policies in the banking industry. At this point I was called in as a consultant to help the department build a culture of effective knowledge management in order to demonstrate knowledge sharing behaviors and to re-create a positive climate throughout the bank.

Green Capital Bank started appreciative sharing of knowledge or ASK methodology out of sheer necessity. The number of changes happening (and still happening) to the banking industry was significant, creating various forms of new knowledge (procedures, rules, technology, etc.) as well as the need to better acquire and share new processes and employee learning.

The Challenge

Keeping employees at the cutting edge of knowledge in the banking field is no small feat. In the late 1990s, financial services technology and operations had become extremely sophisticated with the institution of centralized loan centers, "bank by phone" services, and 24-hour automatic teller machines, as well as the advent of Internet banking and investing. At the same time, employees were still expected to provide top-notch, individualized, face-to-face customer service for clients whenever possible with a more traditional or conservative approach. Obviously, sharing knowledge was vital to maintain Green Capital Bank's competitive edge and sustained financial health.

New knowledge sharing challenges arose as a result of the various mergers Green Capital Bank had undertaken. As redundant employees left the organization, vast amounts of information and knowledge—company history, client relationships, and wisdom gained by experience—left with them. Many of the remaining employees did not feel comfortable sharing their knowledge because they were afraid that doing so would make them more vulnerable to replacement or downsizing *vis-a-vis* their colleagues. Therefore, they began (1) to hoard knowledge to establish a competitive advantage over employees with similar positions and responsibilities, (2) to protect personal turf by keeping knowledge to themselves, becoming a "much needed expert," and (3) to create a perception that with so much extra work after the mergers little time was left to share knowledge. In the words of one employee, "We see [knowledge sharing] as critical, but time-consuming. Sharing is highly valuable, but we just don't have the time to do it."

Green Capital Bank's organizational learning department recognized these challenges to meeting their goal of corporate-wide knowledge sharing. They also realized that knowledge sharing could not be mandated, that is, they could not force people to change. A corporate culture that didn't provide incentives to share knowledge had to change, so the real question became: How does one create a new knowledge-sharing culture as quickly and painlessly as possible? In Green Capital Bank, the ASK process set out to address this challenge of knowledge management.

The Retrospective and Prospective Approaches To Knowledge Management

Knowledge management paradigms can be differentiated as *retrospective* or *prospective*. The former looks back at what happened with a more or less critical, analytical mindset, like a postmortem of an event or a case study. The latter anticipates what kind of knowledge sharing is possible.

The retrospective approach has certain obvious merits. Clearly the traditional, dominant approach, it has been historically used in a wide range of fields. Examples include the case study of a patient in medical schools, the After Action Review [AAR] the U.S. Army uses immediately following a training or practice engagement in the field, and the standard case study approach used in business schools worldwide. The retrospective approach in knowledge management looks at what is dysfunctional in an organization's knowledge use, isolates the causes, and recommends remedial actions or "fixes" to correct the inefficiencies in the system.

While appearing objective, data based, and tangible, the retrospective approach tends to generate costly and damaging fissures in the morale and organizational climate. Engaging in an analysis of what went wrong without assigning responsibility is extremely difficult. As soon as that process begins, the organizational climate is polluted with a wave of "blame gaming."

The prospective approach, on the other hand, does not analyze what went wrong but considers what an individual, group, or

organization must do to reach a desired state or achieve a specific vision. Applied to the knowledge management domain, this approach raises the question, "What must this organization do for its personnel to share their knowledge?" The prospective approach purposely focuses on a new and ever-changing future of information exchange, thus increasing opportunities for harmonious knowledge sharing and proliferation at every level in an organization.

The retrospective and prospective approaches to knowledge management derive some elements of the "learned helplessness" and "learned optimism" concepts popularized by noted psychologist Martin Seligman in the late 1960s and early1990s. In his experiments (Seligman, Maier, & Geer, 1968) when laboratory dogs were given an electric shock, they tried to escape the shock by jumping over to another chamber but found that the bar separating the chambers was too high. After a few repetitions, the height of the bar was reduced significantly so that any dog could easily jump over. However, to Seligman's surprise, the dogs no longer jumped, instead resigning themselves to continuing shocks and the resulting pain.

Based on subsequent, more rigorous research, Seligman argued that exposure to uncontrollable negative events can lead people to believe in their inability to control important outcomes, resulting in a loss of motivation and a failure to act. The internal "understanding" that one cannot control important events tends to lower persistence, motivation, self-esteem, and initiative.

Two decades later another event prompted Seligman to look at the experiment in a different way. In his best selling book *Learned Optimism* (1990), Seligman shows that, based on individual *explanatory styles*[7], one person may see despair in a situation while another sees hope in the same situation. He researches entrepreneurs who, unlike his laboratory subjects, do not give up after several successive failures but rejuvenate after each failure, learning from them and eventually succeeding in their businesses. Seligman shows that such people continuously reframe their reality into possibilities as opposed to limitations, thereby developing "learned optimism."

The retrospective problem-solving approach to knowledge management bears some resemblance to learned helplessness. In the retrospective approach, the consultant, looking at the causes of the failure in knowledge sharing, tends to focus on what cannot be done. In contrast, the prospective approach questions the modalities of reframing. Therefore, the client system must be helped to look at the current status of knowledge sharing using an explanatory style of learned optimism so that they may see the organizational environment as full of possibilities rather than limitations.

Another distinguishing feature of the retrospective approach to knowledge management is the prolific presence of defensive routines, an organizational process first articulated by the well-known organizational learning theorist Chris Argyris (1990). A defensive routine is an institutionalized, ongoing, and routinized mixed message about which discussion is taboo. This elaborate double bind seeks to prevent embarrassment, threat, and awkward situations, thereby maintaining the status quo and avoiding unwanted change. Because organizational defensive routines are intended to avoid the experience of embarrassment, they make it unlikely that the organization will ever genuinely address the factors contributing to the lack of knowledge sharing. This is true even if external knowledge management consultants are brought in. In the prospective approach to knowledge sharing, the consultant does not try to solve or fix the defensive routines. Instead, the focus is on creating open communication, dialogue, and genuine inquiry.

A consultant using the prospective approach is not interested in identifying or isolating the defensive routines suggested by Argyris, because, according to social constructionist theory, paying attention to such constructs only brings them to life with increased intensity. The more the participants talk about the defensive routines, the more they recognize them. The outcome may be a stage of learned helplessness in which they discover that no matter how hard they try, the roadblocks remain and they have virtually no influence in changing them.

The alternative approach in appreciative sharing of knowledge is therefore to focus on harmony or flow rather than defensive routines. By intentionally probing for solid data where knowledge sharing happened, the prospective ASK approach isolates the knowledge enablers rather than the disablers.

Table 2.1 provides the highlights of the retrospective and prospective approaches to knowledge management. Obviously, one is based on a deficit view of knowledge management and the other on a more affirmative view.

Retrospective	Prospective
• **Problem Solving**	• **Appreciative Sharing of Knowledge [ASK]**
• Identify problem	• Value and appreciate "what is"
• Highlight what is broken	• Affirm what is working
• Identify knowledge management problems: **What makes people hoard knowledge?**	• Identify knowledge enablers: **What makes people share knowledge?**
• Analyzing causes	• Envisioning what is possible
• Generating possible solutions	• Generating future-present scenarios
• Action planning and treatment	• Innovating/realizing what will be
• Fixing as intervention	• Affirmation as intervention
• Looking at what is missing	• Looking at what is present
• Managing knowledge as a problem to be solved	• Managing knowledge as an opportunity to be embraced
• Focusing on degenerative diagnosis	• Focusing on generative prognosis
• Focusing on deficiencies	• Focusing on proficiencies
• Responding reactively	• Responding proactively and reflectively
• Focusing on what's urgent	• Focusing on what's important
• Leveraging *learned helplessness*	• Leveraging *learned optimism*
• Passive, cognitive re-affirming of status-quo and current reality	• Active, intentional cognitive re-framing of current reality
• Modernistic	• Postmodern
• Reductionistic	• Social constructionist
• Defensive routines	• Communicating/dialoguing openly
• Managing based on lessons from the past	• Managing based on images of the future

Table 2.1 Contrasting Retrospective and Prospective Approaches to Knowledge Management

Overcoming Initial Reluctance

At Green Capital Bank, the idea of an appreciative approach—starting with proficiencies rather than deficiencies (the prospective approach)—was not immediately embraced by the department. In fact, a handful of Green Capital Bank employees viewed the concept with considerable skepticism. Their apprehension was not unexpected or unreasonable; much of our society operates counter to the prospective concept. Typically, quality experts check for insufficient quality, mechanics look for problems with our automobiles, and consultants strive to identify companies' shortcomings. Somehow, social sciences in general and psychology in particular have ended up with the view that human beings typically lack something.

Over the last century psychology has focused almost entirely on pathology and deficits. Following the science of medicine, it has modeled itself on diagnosing disease.[8]

Furthermore, while the core team understood inherently what it meant to "appreciate,"[9] they needed to gain a deeper understanding of how the process of appreciation works in order to apply it to the project within the bank. The consultant first needed to address their apprehension and to explain the benefits of an "appreciative mind set." He used a hypothetical example of how two people may look at similar paintings—one at an art museum and the other at a flea market. Assuming neither person is an art critic, the person at the art museum is likely to have a better appreciation of the painting than the person viewing a similar painting at the flea market. Because she is in the art museum, she has an appreciative mindset—intentionally looking for beauty in the details, looking hard to see what might have made the experts see the painting as worthy of being placed in the museum. As she looks intently, she sees aspects of the painting someone with a casual mindset at a flea market might miss. Because of the appreciative context, an interpretation that the painting is "beautiful" or "exquisite," is more likely to result.

Applying this principle to the knowledge sharing process, the consultant explained that the group could use an AI method with Green Capital Bank employees to find and expand the pockets of knowledge sharing that were already occurring. By focusing on the present successes in knowledge sharing (rather than failures)—the way the art museum visitor focused on the painting's beauty—already supported and existing knowledge sharing details could be uncovered in the culture. With the awareness of what enabled employees to share what they knew, coupled with the energy generated from the realization of what was already being done well, employees could discover new possibilities and could set their own action items to build a new culture that emphasizes the existence of knowledge sharing programs.

The AI approach then made sense to the team. They realized that the approach would not put people on the spot—neither finger pointing nor blaming would obscure the process. Rather it would allow all employees to share whatever they knew, regardless of perceived significance. They recognized that the best way to capitalize on tacit and distributed knowledge would be to encourage people to share it in whatever way they were comfortable with, rather than in ways that were mandated by upper levels of hierarchy. Green Capital Bank decided to use the AI approach to knowledge management in the organizational learning department, betting that the momentum and lessons learned would spread to the rest of the organization.

Naming the Process

Together we reached a break-through in seeing the issue of knowledge management in the bank in a new light. Though the staff was originally keen on using the After Action Review [AAR] approach of the U.S. Army, after deliberating on the relative merits of the retrospective and prospective approaches, they decided to try the latter one. They based their decision on their desire to try a new approach, one that they thought was innovative and inviting and likely to elicit participation from a majority of bank employees.

At this point the staff deliberated on the most appropriate name for the process. They noted that the term "manage" was associated with hierarchy, and they believed that their challenge was not to manage knowledge—which they recognized would be impossible—but to share it productively. They felt that their focus was more on *sharing* than on *managing* knowledge. Thus, the name *ASK*, or *appreciative sharing of knowledge* was chosen.

Chapter Summary

This chapter briefly introduces the situation faced by the sample organization, Green Capital Bank [GCB] and the process that was used in coming up with a new methodology of knowledge management. The chapter provides a detailed discussion of the two approaches to knowledge management: retrospective and prospective. Though the two approaches appear contradictory, both approaches have their place in the field of knowledge management. In certain situations the retrospective, problem-solving approach might work better. The focus of the book is therefore not in negating the retrospective approaches but in suggesting that the prospective, *appreciative sharing of knowledge* [ASK] approach may generate results that are long lasting and create less alienation and ill will among employees. The resistance to change will be much less in the prospective approach, because no one receives blame for anything that may have gone wrong. Instead, participants are invited to share their excitement and passion for work, proactively contributing whatever they can to make their visions come true. All employees have something of value in the ASK approach that they can share for the common good of the organization and for their own satisfaction.

Practitioner Focus Box

- Study the latest thinking on knowledge management and AI.
- Look at the strengths of various approaches.
- Compare the relative advantages of ASK with the rest.
- Make a decision as to whether ASK will fit your particular situation.

Chapter 3

Setting the Stage for Appreciative Sharing

The Green Capital Bank organizational learning department staff decided unanimously to use appreciative sharing of knowledge [ASK]. There was considerable energy and anticipation for getting started. At the same time, the learning department staff recognized that since ASK entails reframing the way they look at knowledge management, keeping everyone on board was essential. They also realized that, as part of the process, hearing the voices of everyone was also crucial, although employees could not be forced to share knowledge just because of a management decision. Therefore, management invited everyone in Green Capital Bank's organizational learning department to take part in a pilot ASK process.

Step 1: Setting the Stage for ASK

When an organization invites a consultant in, the work of setting the stage actually has begun. Nonetheless, the bulk of the work still remains. Generally, as an introduction to the process "putting the staff through their paces" is beneficial. Active participation in a pilot program allows group members to fully participate, ultimately, learning as they go.

Initiating ASK

Initiating the ASK, or appreciative sharing of knowledge, requires four primary steps.

1. Support the group in examining, understanding, and making the decision to initiate a positive approach to information sharing through ASK.

   A consultant can best accomplish this step not by directly stating that ASK is the proper solution, but by exploring with the client at least three important approaches to knowledge management and change and then leaving the decision to the client. However, a consultant's revealing a predisposition for ASK is entirely appropriate, while at the same time ensuring a willingness to abide by the emerging consensus. The consultant should suggest a pilot program for enabling the staff to experience the process.
2. Design and hold a "pilot event."

   A pilot process allows the consultant and the group to identify and share active examples of knowledge sharing and to analyze and discuss what makes these activities of knowledge sharing possible.
3. Create an on-going process of integrating what they learned in the pilot event.

   This process of integration allows the participants to open themselves to new possibilities and to willingly adopt emerging designs or processes that might be more immediately suitable than those previously planned.
4. Sustain the momentum.

   Submitting, with confidence and optimism, the information gathered through the pilot event to the decision making group is essential to securing top management support for a full ASK process in the key parts of or throughout the entire organization.

The Outcomes of the Pilot

The pilot process ("learning as you go") creates a positive experience to build on for the future organization-wide ASK process. A successful pilot generates self-confidence within the staff and the consultant, enabling them to pursue a process that many in an organization might otherwise characterize as too soft or "touchy feely." The pilot helps the participants discover that change can happen in a "non-traditional," that is, "typical business" way.

To have naysayers question the ASK method should be expected. In such "natural" moments of skepticism, starting with a pilot encourages a shift in the mindset of the doubters. When the bank staff considered the benefits of having as many people participate in the event as possible, they knew it would be an opportunity to uncover organization-wide examples of current detrimental practices at all levels of Green Capital Bank.

Deciding on the Role of Internal Change Agents

During the pilot process the group recognized the need for additional "hands" during the organization-wide event. Green Capital Bank debated whether to hire additional consultants to facilitate or to train internal people to work with the large number of employees who accepted the invitation to participate in the ASK event. The bank chose to use their own employees because they believed that would help in capacity building within the bank, leading to better acceptance of the method in the long run. Green Capital Bank, like many other organizations, had seen consultants coming in, doing their interventions, and then leaving without having transferred enough of their knowledge to sustain change. In addition, using internal staff would save money.

To impart the ASK training, a daylong workshop was organized for 16 Green Capital Bank staff selected by the bank. The day's content and process were designed as a condensed version of what the team would run at the forthcoming organization-wide, two-day event. The overriding goal of the one-day workshop was to train these 16 employees as competent and confident facilitators for the two-day event.

The trained facilitators for the project became known as *knowledge ambassadors*. The ambassadors helped conduct the two-day meeting and played an ongoing role in keeping the process alive and growing over time. The knowledge ambassadors introduced the concept of appreciative sharing of knowledge to the rest of the employees using more or less the same materials the consultant used to introduce the concept to the facilitators previously.

This process, called *emergence* in postmodern literature, is a common occurrence in generative approaches such as appreciative sharing of knowledge, signifying that an organization can't absolutely predict or control how the ASK process unfolds. While the expansion of the scope of the ASK process is the desired development, an organization might require more resources to accommodate the increased participation from a larger stakeholder base.

Chapter Summary

This chapter considers two important questions for any ASK process: (1) How does an organization set the stage for an ASK initiative? and (2) What considerations must they take into account for the greatest organizational participation? Experience suggests the answers lie first in getting a strong buy-in from top management and then in involving as many internal staff as possible to plan and run the ASK process.

A bottom-up approach to ASK, while possible, is less efficient than starting with a top-down approach of strong management support. Generally, the outcome of an ASK project needs some strategic decisions on the part of the management. Likewise, clearly communicating expectations from various partners, including the client and the consultant, is essential. Such communication must recognize the emergent properties of the ASK process, that is, the very real possibility of an escalation of commitment from various stakeholders leading to renewed enthusiasm about being part of the ASK process.

Since ASK is a fundamentally different way of engaging in knowledge management within business organizations, starting with a pilot project is a necessary practical starting point. Success with the pilot creates considerable momentum for expanding the approach throughout the organization incrementally or uniformly. Furthermore, recruiting a cadre of knowledge ambassadors within the organization is essential because they act as internal champions for the project and provide valuable support with the seven steps in ASK.

Practitioner Focus Box

Steps taken before the organizational event

- Locate upper management support for the project.
- Present the ASK paradigm and negotiate top management commitment and support and enroll local informal leaders.
- Train company personnel to act as knowledge ambassadors.

Setting the stage for ASK can be a huge challenge to the practitioner, yet it is vital to integrate the concept into the culture of the organization from the top down. Without buy-in from top management and the success of a pilot, the ASK process might languish in small units, even with positive results. An approach such as ASK requires high visibility in order to create a critical mass of believers or champions who will make a difference in the end by "walking the talk" on knowledge sharing, just as the organizational learning department in Green Capital Bank did.

Chapter 4

Appreciative Sharing of Knowledge (ASK) in Action

How an event opens is key to what it will accomplish. To a large extent, the opening sets the stage for expectations, especially for a new tool such as appreciative sharing of knowledge [ASK] which, at the time Green Capital Bank began considering its implementation, did not have a track record of accomplishments to reassure skeptical participants. In this case, the bank established a powerfully positive context for success by the process of choosing ASK and by its strong statement of support from leadership that they would "go all the way" with the process. Both contextualizing actions were crucial. After a speech from Green Capital Bank's management at the Senior Vice President level advocating the process and encouraging full participation, the department began the main purpose of the event—appreciative sharing of knowledge. Step 2, described below, involved each employee "interviewing" another to hear his or her stories about knowledge sharing currently happening at Green Capital Bank.

Step 2: Eliciting Positive Stories of Successful Knowledge Sharing Behaviors Already Occurring Through Paired Interviews

The ASK process begins with an appreciative process to discover examples of the identified topic: knowledge sharing. The process utilizes an appreciative interviewing process in which all participants within a department divide into pairs and interview their partners to hear stories about knowledge sharing currently happening. Next, the department shares the highlights of the stories from the pairs.

Interview Questions

The consultant carefully selects interview questions, paying particular attention to the context of the project. If the client is interested in a specific aspect of knowledge management, then the consultant customizes the question below to reflect the appropriate emphasis. Otherwise, interviewers ask a question about knowledge sharing in general, as shown below. Vitally important is keeping in mind that the focus of the interviews is intentionally on events and incidents in which knowledge sharing occurs.

1) Think about a few recent positive experiences you have had in this organization with respect to knowledge sharing. Describe one such event when you felt most excited, valued, or appreciated.

   Follow-up questions

   a) What made it a significant positive experience? Or, what is it about the experience that you continue to cherish?
   b) What did you learn from that experience?

2) Name a recent event in which one of your colleagues did something exemplary (outstanding/highly successful) with respect to knowledge sharing. What did he or she do?

   Follow-up questions

   a) What did you admire in her/him?
   b) How has that (what he or she did) contributed to the success of the organization?

Getting a full description of incidents always is important. Each interviewer should take at least 15 minutes for a total of 30 minutes for this interview process. Each interviewer must steer the interview so as to hear more about WHAT happened than WHY it happened. "What" questions typically generate data and understanding, while "why" questions generally elicit an emotional response and generate interpretation as opposed to data. "What" questions tend to make respondents more comfortable, while "why" questions create apprehension and hesitation. Organizers should not allow questions about justification of actions, so that storytellers can share openly without fear of criticism or need for justification.

Identifying Knowledge Sharing Behaviors

Green Capital Bank took the step of identifying knowledge sharing behaviors that were already occurring at their two-day ASK event, held at a bright and welcoming conference center.

When the first day began, hope was running high for many participants. Others, however, were quietly skeptical that the event would become yet another top-down mandated initiative. A few employees greeted the event with a fair amount of cynicism—expecting that change would last only as long as the event itself. Participants in the conference were seated ten to a table with members of their own business unit and one or two trained knowledge ambassadors. The latter encouraged interviewees to tell the story with full details and reminded interviewers to ask "what" questions rather than "why."

The interviewers practiced active listening, a way of communicating that provides a "mirror." This method allows the respondents to hear what they said, thus offering an opportunity to clarify or be further understood. Active listening includes not questioning the validity of the responses but showing explicit, unconditional respect for what the interviewees share. Both the interviewee and the interviewer naturally engage in some problem solving without realizing it, hence, the intentional or mindful focus on what worked as opposed to what did not. In this case, with the help of the knowledge ambassadors, interviewers actively created a nonjudgmental climate for conversation during the interviews.

For example, one staff member talked about the nature of the customer complaints she received in the call center and how she designed a process to handle them on the spot. The interviewer did not ask why complaints were occurring in the first place, why there was a need for training, or why the call center staff was not previously trained in handling difficult callers. Instead, the focus was on finding what she did by the interviewer engaging in a series of "what happened next" questions and by repeating her answers to receive confirmation that she had heard correctly and understood. Each "what happened next" or "what did you do" or "tell me more about it" question led to the unfolding of a layer of information about specific knowledge sharing practices. Some participants began slowly, observing other pairs in action. Others squirmed in their seats, uncomfortable with the word "story," which initially sounded unbusiness-like or not bottom-line-oriented. Yet, within a few minutes, the ballroom buzzed with intense conversation. The observers could see and hear the excitement mounting.

Chapter Summary

In Step 2, participants engaged in the important step of generating positive stories about knowledge sharing in Green Capital Bank. This is not only a required process to transition into the next stage of identifying knowledge enablers, but also a significant sociable and affirmative narrative process. Instead of using a strictly defined protocol of interview questions, ASK used the "story telling" or "narrative" approach, which has become one of the most accepted approaches for data generation in knowledge management today.[10] The World Bank, the international development organization, is famous for championing the story telling approach along with several other practitioners in the field. By asking participants to share publicly stories of their most successful experiences involving knowledge sharing, and by capturing them in a group format, this step created a rich, accessible pool of data that could be analyzed in the next stage for identifying knowledge enablers.

Practitioner Focus Box

- Through paired interviews, elicit positive stories of successful knowledge sharing behaviors already occurring.
- By bringing attention to what is already working in the system, the process reduces the resistance to change typically present in most change efforts. As pointed out earlier, employees might be hesitant to share because of the fear that if everything is shared, they may become expendable. The sharing of stories tends to show an opposite possibility, that is, by sharing they tend to gain both at the individual and organizational level.
- The sharing of "going the extra mile" stories clearly brings about a strong affirmation between the individuals in the pair and leaves them highly energized to move forward.

Chapter 5

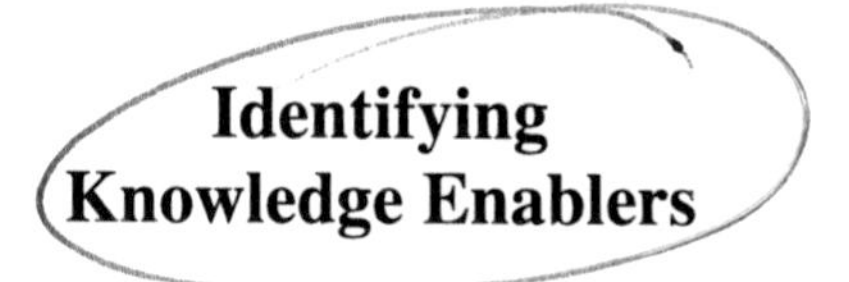

Identifying Knowledge Enablers

Step three in appreciative sharing of knowledge [ASK] is purposely identifying known and unknown knowledge enablers [KE]. The importance of this process cannot be emphasized enough: knowledge enablers are the building blocks of desired and productive knowledge sharing. Knowledge enablers vary from organization to organization, though some of their aspects, like respect or valuing others, appear to be universal enablers to help people share knowledge.

A key question necessary for recognizing knowledge enablers is: *What makes it possible to share knowledge, that is, what "enables" people to be open to participating in this process?* As the term "knowledge enablers" literally indicates, the goal is to identify the kind of processes, values, beliefs, and competencies that encourage, prompt, facilitate, or cause stakeholders in an organization to share the knowledge they possess. A primary impediment to knowledge sharing is that some employees may not even believe that their knowledge is of value to anyone else. Through the process of recognizing and putting knowledge enablers "to work," people in an organization feel more connected with others and with their organizations.

In the ASK process, the focus is on identifying unique attributes of an organization's existing knowledge sharing. For example, what are the values or competencies that currently exist in the organization that, if removed, will fundamentally change the flow or character of knowledge sharing? Or, what are the non-negotiable aspects that, if left unattended or ignored, will lead to a gradual or even precipitous decline in knowledge sharing?

A typical example of a knowledge enabling behavior is *respect*. In a moderately hierarchical organization, like a large investment-banking firm, members take great care in valuing everyone's input, regardless of whether an employee is a mailroom clerk, a junior analyst, or a Vice President. If a junior analyst, for instance, is respected for her research reports even though she does not have the lengthy experience of senior analysts, she is eager and highly committed to contribute to the success of the organization by sharing what she knows. However, if she feels unwanted or insecure, her motivation to share is limited.

Step 3: Identifying Knowledge Enablers

Once the interviews are completed, ask the participants to share the stories they heard from their partners. As they do this public sharing, do not ask justifying questions; simply accept whatever they share and thank them for doing so. During the interview sharing, capture the key themes on a white board. Do not spend too much time wordsmithing—give a name to whatever theme stands out from a story and add it to the white board list. Identifying these themes is crucial to the ASK process.

Locating the Key Themes

Make a first cut or merging of the themes to generate, perhaps, a dozen by grouping similarly named or inter-related themes. For instance, honesty, trust, and trustworthiness might be categorized under "Trust." With the help of the participants, look at the listed themes again and narrow the list to four from the original dozen. In an ASK project, these themes are called knowledge enablers [KE]. As mentioned earlier, they are the building blocks of knowledge sharing, literally enabling the knowledge sharing process.

While certain attributes appear regularly in organizations, every group or organization has its unique combination of knowledge enablers that reflects that organization's particular values. Because the group itself has identified and reached consensus about them, "wrong" answers are not really an issue.

After the Green Capital Bank interview pairs shared their stories, the larger group at the table shared the highlights of the stories from the pairs with the facilitation of the knowledge ambassadors. The stories were filled with real-life examples of moments of knowledge sharing within Green Capital Bank.

- A customer service director at the loan center recounted how she had received communication techniques to help frustrated customers.
- A program supervisor in the training department shared how information from the Branch business unit helped him set up more effective educational programs.
- A new hire in the investment division told how a fellow employee went the extra mile and spent hours after work to show her the ins and outs of the Green Capital Bank investment analysis software.

As participants shared their success stories, growing enthusiasm replaced initial reluctance to talk or to share. A palpable sense of energy overtook each table, and even those who admitted to initial skepticism toward yet another company initiative became highly involved. As the stories were repeated, the knowledge ambassador for each group captured the themes on a flip chart. General themes such as honesty, empowerment, recognition, respect, teamwork, valuing others, and building relationships appeared, thus identifying the "knowledge enablers," that is, the conditions, policies, or behaviors present when knowledge was shared. Participants listened intently and began noticing additional themes and trends in the responses. Green Capital Bank organizational members began to discover, define, and then come to consensus about the knowledge enablers that they recognized as most effective and wanted to cultivate in their organization.

Narrowing the List

With nearly one hundred people at ten tables, the ten flip charts showed long lists of themes. Led by the knowledge ambassadors, the table groups condensed their lists of themes into four or five, being as inclusive as possible. Without a short list, it would be difficult to staying focused on a strategy and assigning responsibility later in the process for various implementation issues would be terribly difficult. Consequently, the groups at the tables analyzed their lists to determine which themes were most important to and most commonly experienced by the group.

The knowledge ambassadors led the process to make a first cut of the themes by grouping similarly named or inter-related themes. For instance, as noted earlier, honesty, trust, and trustworthiness were categorized under Trust. Participants actively narrowed the list to the following four themes.

Knowledge Enabler 1: Empowerment

Empowerment is evident when individuals in an organization gradually acquire the autonomy, freedom, and authority to make appropriate decisions within the domain of their influence. In Green Capital Bank, the overwhelming evidence showed that when employees felt empowered they shared what they knew and listened to others more readily.

For example, an employee designed a distance education-training module and shared what she had done directly with her colleagues across bank divisions. Her supervisor was proud to see his staff take such initiative and felt that, as more of his staff acted to initiate changes, more knowledge sharing would happen in his division.

Knowledge Enabler 2: Respect

Respect is present when individuals are affirmed and granted a certain degree of recognition based on their accomplishments or contribution to the organization. Respect involves noticing, as objectively as possible, what an individual has done, without resorting to the filters of stereotypes based on race, gender, and other forms of difference. Respect demonstrates an active and mindful process of valuing without stereotypical judging.

In Green Capital Bank, respect emerged as an energizing force from the stories shared in the interviews. For example, a woman participant from a minority ethnic group had felt disrespected and undervalued by management until her manager took the time to sit down and talk with her and learn what she had done. As the conversation progressed, the manager began to understand and appreciate the contributions she had made to the group that had gone unnoticed. Through his acknowledgement of the value the individual had added to the group, the manager showed respect, which in turn made the employee feel that she belonged to the group. To her, this was a sign of respect, which in turn prompted her to share more knowledge with her manager and her entire team since then. From this position of acceptance, the employee was motivated to share more deliberately the tacit knowledge she had picked up over the years.

Knowledge Enabler 3: Teamwork

Teamwork is the process of working well together in a group that has formed voluntarily or by design. This process enables the pooling of various intangible resources of individual members such that collective knowledge is greater than that generated by the simple combining of individual knowledge.

In the organizational learning department of Green Capital Bank, teamwork was a time-tested concept. The stories shared exhibited a level of genuineness that clearly wasn't manufactured "for display." For example, a team member involved in a project with her teammates reported a great deal of communication within her team, including weekly teleconferences providing pre-meeting information sharing, at which everyone's ideas were welcome. With the team actively keeping open lines of communication, their efforts resulted in an accessible team in which any member could call anyone anytime and get a friendly welcoming response. Eventually, the project turned out to be a massive, cross-market project whose success was largely the result of highly efficient teamwork, facilitated by knowledge sharing.

Knowledge Enabler 4: Building Relationships

Building relationships is an element of what has recently been called *social capital formation*. Robert Putnam (2001) defined social capital as the features of social organization such as networks, norms, and social trust that facilitate coordination and cooperation for mutual benefit, that is, "the sum of the resources, actual or virtual, that accrue to an individual or a group by virtue of possessing a durable network of more or less institutionalized relationships of mutual acquaintance and recognition" (Bourdieu & Wacquant, 1992, p. 119). Social capital is "the set of elements of the social structures that affect relations among people and are inputs for the production and/or utility function" (Schiff, 1992, p. 160). It may be considered the goodwill engendered by the fabric of social relations. A growing body of research in management suggests that social capital is a differentiating variable at individual and group level for career growth and organizational effectiveness. Knowledge sharing stories in the bank clearly pointed toward improved building of relationships. In the story of the new hire who learned about the investment analysis software from a colleague, both the experienced organizational member and the newcomer developed a friendship that led to further knowledge sharing between them as an ongoing process.

Identifying Common Knowledge Enablers

The knowledge ambassadors from each table then shared their lists so everyone in the room could hear the summary of themes. While each table had its own special combination of knowledge enablers, commonalities appeared across tables. As noted above, the four knowledge enablers common to the larger group were *empowerment, respect, teamwork,* and *relationship building*. In a setting like the Green Capital Bank, where a large number of stakeholders are involved, creating a consensus around the eventually chosen knowledge enablers is absolutely vital. Individual groups or divisions, of course, get attached to their own knowledge-enabler terms and want to see them as the chosen KEs. Green Capital Bank had a relatively smooth process of deciding upon the common enablers. However, it is possible, even likely, to have a situation in which consensus formation may be time-consuming and engaging.

Timing

From the appreciative knowledge management perspective, the knowledge enablers were extremely important for knowledge sharing to happen in Green Capital Bank's organizational learning department. The entire process, from asking the first interview question to finding the four common themes of the entire room, took only two hours. Not only did the group determine what makes sharing knowledge possible and probable, they had modeled the actual act of knowledge sharing through the process of utilizing the Appreciative Inquiry [AI] process.

As is often the case, at the end of this segment, participants indicated surprise at the amount of successful knowledge sharing that had been happening unnoticed within Green Capital Bank. Therefore, they felt an enthusiastic connection to the common themes discovered at their table.

During the remainder of the two-day event, the focus was for the attendees to understand the interconnection of these factors, what facilitated their existence, and how participants could make them more routine in order to enhance knowledge sharing.

Chapter Summary

This chapter discusses the process and the logic used in identifying the knowledge enablers in the ASK process. The process begins with the stakeholders identifying and sharing positive critical incidents that demonstrate knowledge sharing, followed by the extraction of key ingredients within such stories. They are further distilled into four or five fundamental behaviors known as knowledge enablers.

KNOWLEDGE ENABLERS =
ROOT CAUSE OF SUCCESS

Practitioner Focus Box

Step 3: Identify Knowledge Enablers

- **Practice caution in identifying knowledge enablers (KEs).** This step should be undertaken only after the consultant and the client have developed a deep understanding of what is meant by knowledge enablers. In the absence of an in-depth understanding of what it is and what it is not, several trivial, too general, or inconsequential concepts might get onto the list, which in turn may weaken the rest of the process.

- **Run the "what if" question to confirm the validity of the knowledge enablers.**
  Once you have tentatively identified the knowledge enablers (KE), ask yourself and the client system the question: What would happen if these particular knowledge enablers ceased to exist? Would it lead to a decline in the knowledge sharing processes expressed in the positive stories shared in the earlier Step 2 (where each employee interviewed another to hear his or her stories about knowledge sharing currently happening in the organization)?

- **Run the "word in the street" test to see how the knowledge enabler (KE) term resonates with members of the organization.**
  Remember, organizations are linguistic systems and socially and culturally constituted. The term "respect" may have a strong meaning in one organization but not much currency in another, even if the underlying principle of respect came out as a knowledge enabler in the second organization. In the latter case, you need a different term that is more attuned to the sub-culture of the organization. For example, valuing others might convey the same knowledge-enabling meaning in the second organization as respect conveys in the first. A quick informal check on the "social suitability" of the knowledge-enabler term can be conducted by conferring with a few representatives of the client system.

Chapter 6

Leveraging Knowledge Infrastructure

Once the organization has identified and further explored the knowledge-enabler factors, the remaining task is to enhance the operation of those factors within the system, what some would call the hardest part of the process.

The appreciative sharing of knowledge (ASK) method calls this process the *Galatea effect*. In Greek mythology, Galatea is the statue of a beautiful woman brought to life by Aphrodite, goddess of love, in response to the prayers of the sculptor Pygmalion, who had fallen in love with his creation. A whole body of convincing research documents this phenomenon, alternatively called "self-fulfilling prophecy," Pygmalion effect,[11] or Rosenthal effect (Reynolds, 2002; Rowe and O'Brien, 2002; Kierein and Gold, 2000; Murphy, Campbell, and Garavan, 1999). In the knowledge sharing context, the knowledge enablers are like Galatea, highly desirable and so attractive that people desire to bring them to life or to see more of them in practice in their work settings. In practice, once the organization has identified the knowledge enablers correctly, they can begin building on them by helping individuals imagine the ideal future as if it has already happened.

Step four of the ASK process is designed to build on the knowledge enablers by analyzing them with respect to the organization.

Step 4: Analyze the Data Using Knowledge Infrastructure Factors

Organizations need to think of their knowledge infrastructure factors [KIFs] metaphorically as the interior structural pillars supporting an architectural structure. They are not visible to the human eye from outside, but if the internal structural pillars are removed or damaged, the building will collapse. Yet, when looking at an architectural marvel, viewers do not necessarily focus on the pillars, perhaps not even being aware of their existence: The pillars don't command attention, nor are they very noticeable to the casual external glance. Yet, the pillars are critical for the very existence of the building. The knowledge infrastructure factors work in a similar way. Without them, the knowledge enablers cannot exist.

While knowledge enablers are specific to each individual organization, the knowledge-infrastructure factors are the same for all organizations. For example, collegiality among faculty may be a knowledge enabler for a university although not necessarily for a steel plant. For the latter, respect may be. Spirituality may be a knowledge enabler for a religious order but not for a large Wall Street investment banking firm. However, all four—the university, the steel plant, the religious order, and the Wall Street firm—will have some of the same knowledge infrastructure factors, such as decision making, leadership, and organizational practices. All these organizations will have specific decision-making styles, leaders of various types, and organizational practices and routines.

Organizational practices vary from firm to firm—one may have a weekly staff meeting while another may have a monthly gathering, but they are both valid organizational practices. However, all might not support knowledge sharing. Therefore, identifying those that support the existence of knowledge enablers is critically important for bringing change. A review of knowledge management research literature identifies the following knowledge infrastructure factors: decision-making, organizational practices and routines, incentives for knowledge sharing, leadership, and communication.

Decision-making

As a knowledge infrastructure factor, decision-making refers to the relatively permanent and institutionally legitimized way an organization makes decisions. Over a period of time, based on historicity and norms, organizations tend to develop a pattern of decision-making that old timers transmit to newcomers through socialization processes. Examples include participatory, consensus-based, and autocratic decision making styles.

Organizations will have certain decision-making styles irrespective of the knowledge enablers they have. For example, faculty in a particular university may identify freedom of expression as a knowledge enabler, because they consider freedom of expression a core to knowledge sharing. In a nonprofit development-oriented organization, empowering others may be a knowledge enabler. In both organizations, decision-making is a knowledge infrastructure factor. In either organization, if "management" tries to make decisions autocratically, it will certainly affect freedom of expression among faculty members and the empowering of others in the nonprofit organization.

A significant body of research suggests that participatory or consensus-based decision making styles tend to foster collaborative behavior in organizations[12]. Clearly, collaborative behaviors are more likely to lead to knowledge sharing than competitive practices do. In the latter, individuals may have a vested interest in protecting or hoarding their knowledge. ASK facilitates collaborative behaviors.

Organizational Practices and Routines

Organizational practices refer to routines, procedures, and established ways of doing things that have been socially constructed and become normal, like a habit. They tend to get repeated with certain periodicity; the organizational participants come to anticipate the occurrence of these routines or procedures at the prescribed time and place. All organizations have routines and practices, such as holding a weekly Monday morning meeting, having a welcome party for a new employee, or letting every employee, irrespective of rank, meet with the President if the employee desires.

Several highly functioning knowledge sharing organizations have instituted an organizational practice called *communities of practice* [CoP][13] in which people share their knowledge informally and voluntarily. A CoP used for knowledge sharing might be voluntarily organized on the spur of the moment by those interested in enhancing their knowledge and networking on a certain subject or profession when they recognize a sudden or pressing need. Typically, individuals gather for 40 minutes and share their personal knowledge and at the same time learn new practices and procedures from those who share.

Recent organizational research suggests that organizational routines can have either faciliatory or inhibitive influences on organizational innovation. For example, a practice of having to send every new idea for approval through a chain of hierarchy is most likely to inhibit innovation. On the other hand, a different practice that allows a group that comes up with a new idea to bring it to the production stage may encourage employees to work harder to find creative solutions. When an engineer in Hewlett-Packard refers to the "HP way," he or she is actually referring to its institutionalized practice and routines. HP insiders know what to do when a new idea emerges in their unit. It will lead to a predictable series of actions and follow-ups, even though they may be unaware that they are reacting in a routine manner.

Numerous research studies[14] demonstrate that certain organizational practices like the communities of practice [CoP] strongly facilitate knowledge sharing and enhance change. Other evidences point to the long term advantages of productive organizational routines. Once established, they are relatively easy to maintain, thereby freeing up valuable organizational energy for more proactive strategies and actions.

Recognizing that habits, routines, and norms can be either a liability or an asset is very important. Once solidified with time, habits and routines, whether productive or non-productive, tend to become comfortable and institutionalized. In that context, the ASK process gives a unique opportunity for stakeholders to see if the routines are facilitating or inhibiting knowledge enabling. If they are inhibiting it, the future-present scenarios [FPS] introduced later in the book offer a pragmatic way to address the situation.

Incentives, leadership, and communication are the remaining knowledge infrastructure factors. Together with decision-making and organizational practices and routines, they constitute the support structure that not only maintains the knowledge enablers but also enhances them when used as key elements of the future-present scenario construction process, explained in the next chapter.

Incentives for Knowledge Sharing

Socially constructed organizational practices and routines, whether positive or negative, eventually shape the type of incentives for knowledge sharing.

Incentives as a knowledge infrastructure factor are benefits—material and psychological rewards—that the organization institutionalizes to encourage knowledge sharing. A key question is: What incentives are in place to recognize individuals who share knowledge? All organizations have incentives that may or may not encourage knowledge sharing.

The impact of incentives on organizational performance has been thoroughly researched and documented. Available evidence suggests that both material and psychological incentives play a key role in employee morale and satisfaction. In some cases, financial incentives cease to have an impact, and intangible ones, like status, challenge, autonomy, recognition, etc., become more important. As a knowledge infrastructure factor [KIF], most incentives are likely to be psychological rather than material or financial.

Leadership

Not surprisingly, leadership is a knowledge infrastructure factor. Leadership is a critical structural element for all organizations. Some leadership styles support knowledge enablers better than others. Identifying those that are significant to the group or organization, as noted earlier, is of critical importance. Leadership is one of the most researched concepts in management. Voluminous empirical data and anecdotal evidence are readily available to demonstrate the role of leadership in creating excellence in organizations. In the case of ASK, the support provided by leadership appears to contribute to the legitimacy and acceptance of the process. Such an observation is, of course, consistent with traditional change management literature, which has shown again and again that top management support is critical for change efforts to succeed.

Organizational practices and leadership together impact the possibility of change in knowledge sharing and communication processes—both essential to moving organizations forward. Certain practices, such as the presence of distributed, self-autonomous groups, are likely to encourage the emergence of participative leadership styles. Conversely, the participative leadership style may encourage the creation of self-autonomous groups. While it is not necessary or even possible to determine which comes first, recognition of the mutual causality or interdependence between the two is useful in creating action steps for planning.

Communication

Like leadership, communication is a knowledge infrastructure factor [KIF]. The quality and style of communication that support knowledge sharing are the focus here. Also, just like leadership, communication as a concept is solidly researched and shown to directly influence the quality of organizational outcomes.

Some communication styles enhance knowledge sharing while others curtail it. Research strongly supports what is "common knowledge" to many organizational development practitioners: an open communication style, in which employees can talk to each other without regard to hierarchical status, tends to create a knowledge-sharing climate. In contrast, organizations with set rules about channels of communication and strict protocols regarding who can talk to who tend to generate a climate in which people are far less likely to take the time or the risk of sharing.

As in the case of leadership, organizational practices and routines impact communication styles as well. For example, the higher the number of self-autonomous groups in an organization, the higher the probability of horizontal channels of communication flourishing.

Interdependency of Knowledge Infrastructure Factors and Knowledge Enablers

Recognizing that the above knowledge infrastructure factors are intermingled and interdependent is important. From a constructionist perspective, all labeling (naming) is socially constituted, serving the purpose of aiding the sense-making process. This interdependence suggests that one knowledge infrastructure factor cannot exist without the support and existence of the other. Each promotes the existence of the other; in fact, making sense cannot happen without the existence of the other. Yet, as in many identifying processes, treating them as if they are "independent" makes the data more analyzable and understandable. Further, the possibility of designing proposition statements (explained below) is easier through recognizing that interactivity between the actionable, independent knowledge infrastructure factors and knowledge enablers is vital to productive knowledge sharing.

Building a Knowledge Enabler-Knowledge Infrastructure Matrix at Green Capital Bank

The ASK event at Green Capital Bank made an intentional attempt to put the information into a manageable framework that connected knowledge enablers [KE] with knowledge infrastructure factors [KIF]. The objective is to find ways to enhance the identified knowledge enablers so that knowledge sharing becomes a continuous, sustainable, long-term activity. The ASK team accomplishes this by organizing the interview responses obtained in step 2 (discussed earlier in Chapter 4) into a large matrix with the knowledge enablers on one axis of the matrix list and the infrastructure factors on the other. The cells in the matrix contain examples of the knowledge enablers and knowledge infrastructure factors they represent.

Accordingly, the consultant and change/knowledge ambassadors organized the knowledge enablers, knowledge infrastructure factors, and previously collected success stories into a large table, listing the knowledge enablers across the top of the table and the infrastructure factors along the side. The knowledge ambassadors plastered sticky notes with examples (from the interview stories) into the cells of the matrix. Once each group of participants added its notes, a subset of the table looked like Table 6.1. Many stories overlapped different knowledge enablers and knowledge infrastructure factors. Such unanimity suggested that an underlying set of knowledge enablers were indeed in that organization and that the process thus far was producing valid results.

Knowledge Enablers

Knowledge Infrastructure Factors

	Empowerment	**Teamwork**	**Respect**	**Building relationships**
Decision making	Examples of decision making styles that facilitate empowerment	Examples of decision making styles that facilitate teamwork	Examples of decision making styles that facilitate respect	Examples of decision making styles that facilitate building relationships
Leadership	Examples of leadership styles that facilitate empowerment	Examples of leadership styles that facilitate teamwork	Examples of leadership styles that facilitate respect	Examples of leadership styles that facilitate building relationships
Communities of practice [CoP] & Organizational Practices	Examples of CoPs & OPs that facilitate empowerment	Examples of CoPs & OPs that facilitate teamwork	Examples of CoPs & OPs that facilitate respect	Examples of CoPs & OPs that facilitate building relationships
Incentives	Examples of incentive systems that facilitate empowerment	Examples of incentive systems that facilitate teamwork	Examples of incentive systems that facilitate respect	Examples of incentive systems that facilitate building relationships
Communication	Examples of communication that facilitate empowerment	Examples of communication that facilitate teamwork	Examples of communication that facilitate respect	Examples of communication that facilitate building relationships

Table 6.1 Knowledge Sharing Matrix (Not all knowledge infrastructure factors and knowledge enablers are shown.)

Knowledge Enablers

Knowledge Infrastructure Factors

Knowledge Infrastructure Factors	Empowerment	Respect	Building Relationships
Leadership - Vision - Strategic Focus - Accountabilities		I felt respected and valued after my manager took the time to sit down and talk with me and listened to me with great respect.	
Decision Making - Priorities - Goals	I volunteered for several event responsibilities and shared more with other facilitators when I felt like we were empowered to shape the outcome of the event.	I learned communication techniques from the loan center to help my call center's frustrated customers. I was able to accept more information from them because they showed great respect for my position and because in the end, they let me decide how to handle customers.	Information from the branch business unit helped me set up more effective educational programs.
Organizational Practices - Teams - Cross-LOB teams - Planning process - Hiring - Promotion - Performance - What is valued		I felt valued and affirmed when my manager mentioned my name during the weekly meeting. He shared to the whole group that I was able to finish a certain task against a tight deadline and that he felt very good about what I had accomplished.	Just after I was hired, one of my co-workers spent hours after work to show me the ins and outs of their investment analysis software. I volunteered for several event responsibilities and shared more with other facilitators when I felt like we were empowered to shape the outcome of the event.

Table 6.2 Knowledge Sharing Matrix with Specific Examples (Not all knowledge infrastructure factors and knowledge enablers are shown.)

From this matrix, Green Capital Bank employees made sense of the stories they had heard by identifying trends and patterns of current knowledge sharing. They began to see the evidence of possibilities to expand what they already do well in knowledge sharing. It was an affirmation that significant potential existed in the organization to move forward, making the best use of what they already do well. They recognized the importance of knowledge sharing for the continued growth of the organization in the highly competitive environment in which Green Capital Bank existed. The clear trend, as evidenced in the matrix, gave them the confidence and courage to think strategically about what more might be possible, in concrete terms, to accelerate knowledge sharing in ways that would contribute to the Green Capital Bank's competitive advantage—and long-term existence.

Chapter Summary

This chapter defines, identifies, and describes the various knowledge infrastructure factors [KIFs] that contribute to the enhancement of the knowledge enablers [KEs]. Based on experience and a synthesis of various organizational analysis models, the consultant identified the following knowledge infrastructure factors in this chapter: decision-making, organizational practices and routines, incentives, leadership, and communication. The chapter describes how the participants in the project analyzed the interview data by organizing them into a matrix of knowledge infrastructure factors and knowledge enablers [Tables 6.1 and 6.2]. The analyzed data become the foundation for the subsequent important step of constructing future-present scenarios [FPS]. For this reason, it is important to spend adequate time making sure the data analysis is accurate by having the participant-groups look at each others' analysis, provide constructive feedback, and revise them before starting the next process.

Practitioner Focus Box

Step 4: Analyze the Data Using Knowledge Infrastructure Factors

The most important aspect is generating a fairly reasonable operational definition of what each knowledge infrastructure factor is. By agreeing on an operational definition as opposed to a conceptual one, the likelihood is higher for inter-rater reliability in the data analysis. That is, more agreement is likely between participants regarding what knowledge infrastructure factor a given statement in an interview might be referring to. One way to generate operational definition is to ask coders (people analyzing the data) for examples for each knowledge infrastructure factor based on their experience and beliefs. Once shared, the consultant can help the knowledge ambassadors sort through their differences and come to some consensus regarding what kinds of descriptions they will code as a specific knowledge infrastructure factor.

Not to have data for every cell in the matrix is normal. For example, you may find several examples of the KIF leadership that support the knowledge enabler of respect but not for the KIF communication and knowledge enabler of respect. In such case, simply leave the matrix empty.

Also important is regularly revisiting the operational definitions of knowledge infrastructure factors as the analysis continues. People forget some aspects of the definition and fall back on their everyday understanding of the concept, which, in all likelihood, may be different for each person.

Chapter 7

Moving into the Future with Appreciative Sharing

With the active involvement of its employees and based on concrete evidence, the appreciative sharing of knowledge process first identified the knowledge enablers and the organizational infrastructural factors that supported them at Green Capital Bank.

As important as recognizing the knowledge enablers is sustaining those discovered is crucial. A logical question that emerges at this point is, "How does the organization sustain these knowledge enablers?" Given that entropy—the degradation of energy in a system, leading to inertia— is a natural occurrence in all systems, Green Capital Bank had to find ways to ensure that the knowledge enablers did not become entropic. Organizations must discover methods to continually enhance the enablers, since, based on systems theory, they either decline or grow but do not remain static. By creating a vision of what is possible based on what is already present (as opposed to adding what is absent), the ASK process prevents entropy from occurring through continual enhancement of the knowledge enablers. Doing so creates what ASK calls Future-Present Scenario statements [FPS].

The term *future-present* may appear paradoxical. However, if stakeholders in an organization can think of the future as already present, they will get a better sense of living that future. Therefore, successful change becomes more possible. Imagining a concrete, sometimes immediately realizable future scenario has long been used in sports psychology. Sprinters, for instance, mentally picture themselves crossing the finish line while they are running or preparing to run. According to this view, the difference between saying to oneself "I am going to win" and "I have won" is considerable. Theoretically, the latter produces a more vivid image of the desired end state than the former does, thereby enhancing the competitive energy and leading to improved performance.

Step 5: Construct Future-Present Scenarios [FPS]

Once the organizers have displayed the interview data in the matrix, the next step is constructing future-present scenario [FPS] statements. Research evidence in cognitive psychology now fully supports future-present scenario practices, sometimes called "visualization" exercises. Stated as if the future has come to the present, a future-present scenario statement concretely describes with rich details a future desired state happening now. The key is in the richness of the description. The more details about a future-present scenario one creates, the more concrete the statements become after the writing process. Further, the future-present scenario statements consist of what is possible, with no deficit terms. Cognitive psychologists show that deficit constructs tend to create a deficit or a fragmented reality. By creating a future-present scenario, the stakeholders' minds populate themselves with vivid details of a new reality. Often without being consciously aware, they engage in behaviors likely to produce more or less the same reality that exists in their thoughts.

In the case of ASK, a future-present scenario helps suggest real possibilities for knowledge sharing in the organization. By heightening their attention to such possibilities, it makes them more likely to become reality.

At the same time, the data must support the future-present scenarios. That is, the matrix of knowledge infrastructure factors [KIFs] and knowledge enablers [KEs] has to be the launching pad for the future-present scenario process. Organizers and stakeholders must not use this process as mere wish-fulfillment, just making up a future-present scenario because they like it, wish it to happen, or think it is what the organization needs. For the future actually to happen, stakeholders must tap the potential and strength of the present. The most efficient method to understand and leverage the potential of the present is through a careful data analysis of what the participants have already stated in the previous interviews and other ASK activities.

The Commitment-Inspiration-Groundedness [CIG] Model

As pointed out above, an embeddedness in data meaningful to the process is a distinguishing feature of the appreciative sharing of knowledge process. Embeddedness remains crucial in creating the future-present scenarios that bring continued change. One way to structure this process is to use the commitment, inspiration, and groundedness [CIG] model designed by the consultant. Three elements interact in creating a future-present scenario statement in the model (Figure 7.1).

The consultant creates the commitment, inspiration, and groundedness [CIG] model as a synthesis of several theories of managing change conceptualized by management thinkers and scholars, such as Kurt Lewin (1947, 1951/1997), Douglas McGregor (1960), Abraham Maslow (1954), Frederick Herzberg (1959), Carl Rogers (1961/1995; 1980/1995), and Chris Argyris (1993). They demonstrate that certain elements need to be in place so that individuals, groups, or organizations can change. For example, psychotherapists have long observed that individuals change when their desire for change (aspiration) is synergistically combined with concrete "baby steps" (groundedness) and a plan to stay on course (commitment). If the change is dramatic or the expectations unrealistic, the commitment to sustain the change eventually wavers, diminishes, and then vanishes.

The same can be said of groups and organizations. Change agents must learn the art of both creating enough energy and desire for change as well as grounding the desired new behaviors, practices, or structures in something specific, measurable, and concrete. Above all, they need to think long term, that is, how long can these changes be sustained? Is the stakeholders' commitment sufficient to carry out the change process?

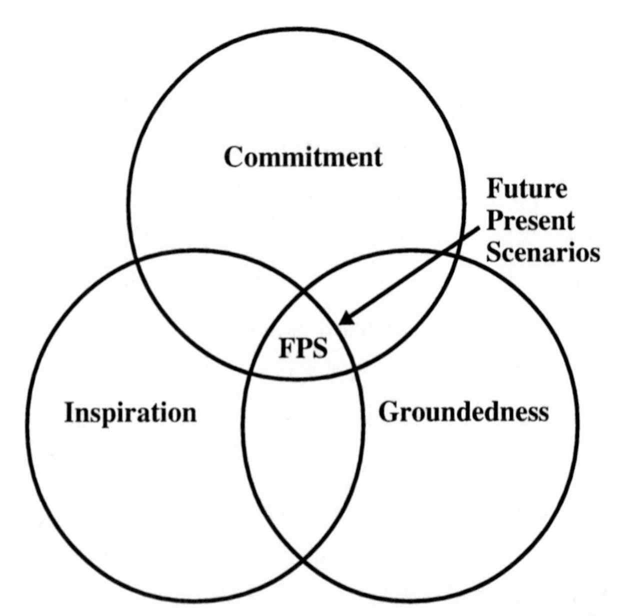

Figure 7.1 Interacting Elements of Future-Present Scenario [FPS] Statements

Commitment, inspiration, and groundedness must be present in a healthy future-present scenario. Without commitment, the new possibility will not materialize. In such a scenario building activity participants can easily come up with provocative or daring possibilities, but a consultant must ask: Does the data so far show evidence of a long-term commitment for making this scenario possible?

The second element in the model, inspiration, is the driver that provides the energy for people to carry out the new possibility. The third element, groundedness, underscores that the future-present scenario must be realistic and plausible. If it is too far-fetched, looking too radical or beyond the capabilities of the organization, not enough stakeholders will have the energy to make it happen. This is a fine line and calls for careful judgment on the part of the participants and consultant. Overall, a future-present scenario constructed using the three elements of commitment, inspiration, and groundedness is more likely to become a reality.

The group must write future-present scenarios for each knowledge enabler and each knowledge infrastructure factor as in the following matrix (similar to the table used in the analysis of knowledge enablers in Step 4, Chapter 6), listing knowledge enablers across the top and knowledge infrastructure factors down the left column.

Knowledge Enablers

Knowledge Infrastructure Factors

	Empowerment	**Teamwork**	**Respect**	**Building relationships**
Decision making	Propositions related to decision making styles that enhance empowerment	Propositions related to decision making styles that enhance teamwork	Propositions related to decision making styles that enhance respect	Propositions related to decision making styles that enhance building relationships
Leadership	Propositions related to leadership styles that enhance empowerment	Propositions related to leadership styles that enhance teamwork	Propositions related to leadership styles that enhance respect	Propositions related to leadership styles that enhance building relationships
Communities of practice [CoP] & Organizational Practices	Propositions related to CoPs & OPs that enhance empowerment	Propositions related to CoPs & OPs that enhance teamwork	Propositions related to CoPs & OPs that enhance respect	Propositions related to CoPs & OPs that enhance building relationships
Incentives	Propositions related to incentive systems that enhance empowerment	Propositions related to incentive systems that enhance teamwork	Propositions related to incentive systems that enhance respect	Propositions related to incentive systems that enhance building relationships
Communication	Propositions related to communication that enhance empowerment	Propositions related to communication that enhance teamwork	Propositions related to communication that enhance respect	Propositions related to communication that enhance building relationships

Table 7.1 Matrix for constructing future-present scenario statements

To create future-present scenarios, groups can consider the following:

1) Locate significant examples of each knowledge enabler, the best of "what is" from the Step 2 matrix.
2) Analyze/interpret how and what kind of knowledge infrastructure factors [KIFs] positively increase or support each knowledge enabler.
3) Extrapolate from the "best of what is" to envision what is possible. Be imaginative and inspiring. Let the resulting creativity envision a collectively desirable future for the organization.
4) Construct a future-present scenario statement of what is possible and state it in affirmative language as if the scenario were already true and happening fully in the present.

Once Green Capital Bank identified their knowledge enablers and understood them in the framework of the bank's infrastructure, building on them was possible by helping individuals imagine the ideal future as if it had already happened. ASK participants constructed the future-present scenario statements for each knowledge enabler and knowledge infrastructure factor. For example: "Staffers have hour-long gatherings every Monday at the Green Capital Bank during which the group members listen to one another, hearing what everyone has to say. This occurs no matter how busy the staff is. At these meetings, staffers share discoveries about the projects in progress, making space for input and concerns of those with information or those with questions. Also, at this gathering staffers discuss what must or could be achieved during the coming week(s) and, again, seek input from others for accomplishing agreed upon goals. Everyone receives specific responsibilities regarding what must be accomplished." A related, second future-present scenario is having Friday afternoons as regular meeting times to take stock of what had been accomplished and what can be learned from these experiences. These are called "weekly reflections."

Writing Future-Present Scenarios

Writing future-present scenarios involves certain criteria (noted below) that help avoid potential ambiguity.

1. Write it as if it is already happening. Use present tense.
2. Be specific. State the activity, skill, or practice you propose to create the new reality.
3. Examine how you feel about living in the new vision and reality.
4. Keep the "Commitment—Inspiration—Grounded-ness" model in mind.

After drafting the future-present scenario statement, consider whether it accommodates the following:

1. Is the statement really challenging or merely a restatement of something already in practice?
2. Is it specific, concrete, and tangible, as opposed to something very general and abstract?
3. Does it inspire you, the participant?
4. Does it stay grounded and connected to the knowledge enabler and the knowledge infrastructure factor under consideration?

Remembering that different organizations create different possibilities based on their own style, culture, preferences, etc. is important. Even the amount of detail or how specific the statements are varies across different organizations. As long as the organization meets the criteria—inspired, committed, and grounded—and the possibilities stretch the current reality, accept whatever future-present scenarios they create. Additionally, accept as many as the group feels it is important to add. The greater the participation in this step (as with every other), the greater the success of the ASK project and the future knowledge sharing within the organization.

After long hours of work, the Green Capital Bank employees finished creating the future-present-scenarios. When asked if they wanted to continue working, the group answered with a definite and positive "yes," demonstrating the continuing high energy from the momentum that had built up during the day. Although they were near the end of the first day of the event, participants were still enlivened. Conversation between tables had opened up, with employees from all business units chatting about productive ways they would work beneficially together after the event. These lively exchanges were punctuated by "why not" and "can we" questions initiating new and innovative ways of achieving together.

Next, using the matrix from for earlier analysis, participants created their own future-present scenarios for each of the knowledge enablers and infrastructure components (Table 7.2). While some of the propositions in the matrix didn't seem extraordinary to some participants, knowledge ambassadors reminded everyone that the statements showed what was possible and desired, but not already occurring. The following table is a subset of the complete matrix created by the group:

Knowledge Enablers

Knowledge Infrastructure Factors

	Empowerment	Respect	Building Relationships
Leadership - Vision - Strategic Focus - Accountabilities	Every employee in the business unit is free to be a leader by being a revolving chairperson for our Friday afternoon meetings.	Leaders show respect by accepting and acting on team members' ideas. Leaders show respect by listening fully and then asking questions rather than contradicting ideas. Trainers are acknowledged by their leaders at June and December program events for contributions with regard to knowledge sharing.	Leaders build relationships by sharing information through meetings and eating lunch with new employees. The trainers work on assigning cross-functional projects that increase cross-functional knowledge. Leaders participate in both informal and formal knowledge sharing through "water cooler" meetings and learning communities; thus teamwork.
Decision Making - Priorities - Goals	Risk taking is encouraged and supported by our unit managers. Trainers are empowered to implement changes to program delivery and share results with peers.	Leaders trust the ideas, experience, knowledge and opinions of staff members and involve them in the decision making process.	Key stakeholders are involved in knowledge sharing activities.
Communication - How people know what others are working on - How knowledge is gained in communication	Employees consistently provide data for the knowledge sharing repository during and after the project, such that it can be used by all.	Staff hold a yearly knowledge fair to communicate what different lines of business are doing. To show respect for each other's work, each line of business is invited to have a booth. All participants visit each booth to find out about others' projects.	Business presentations are shared with all service partners. Staff facilitates various Regional Community Bank programs to educate their service partners. Staff meets with sector managers and coaches on a bi-weekly basis to educate them in the in-branch experience.

Table 7.2 Future-Present Scenarios Matrix with Examples

Ending the Day

The Green Capital Bank employees began to see more than common interests and needs: they saw ways to build a common future of excellence. The day ended with pride about the work they had accomplished as well as curiosity about what would happen the next day.

In response, the organizers held a debriefing at the end of the day. Green Capital Bank employees expressed both excitement and exhaustion, pleased with what they had accomplished but also ready to break for the evening. Afterwards, as consultant, I provided my observations to the organizers, emphasizing the remarkable seriousness and commitment of the staff to create concrete outcomes from the series of activities they had engaged in. In particular, I commented on the absence of blaming or "finger-pointing" of any sort and shared the group's sense of satisfaction in seeing a large number of people working with a clear focus and a common purpose.

Meanwhile, an internal Community of Practice [CoP] group in the Bank planned and organized an after-dinner cultural-entertainment event in a large hall, featuring several skits after dinner. Most of the skits revolved around the theme of appreciative sharing of knowledge as community of practice and made recognizable, often humorous references to the day's activities, employing role-playing and examples of various knowledge enablers and future-present scenarios. This allowed the employees to look at the whole approach as something both fun and meaningful. In addition, the skits maintained continuity for the following day.

Chapter Summary

This chapter discusses the concept of future-present scenarios: their logic, their construction, their special "do's and don'ts," and their consolidation using a model of "commitment, inspiration, and groundedness." The chapter emphasizes the need to spend sufficient time explaining the rationale of future-present scenarios to the participants and helping them understand the difference between wanting to accomplish a goal and the actual state of being there. Having both the elements of inspiration and groundedness in one statement provides mutually enhancing energy to a single action item in such a way that the resulting plan is both bold and doable.

Practitioner Focus Box

Step 5. Construct Future-Present Scenarios (FPS).

- The future-present scenario (FPS) is a powerful and useful concept. It is strongly recommended that consultants spend adequate time explaining the logic of FPS, giving good examples of the three elements of commitment, inspiration, and groundedness.

- Future-present scenarios may be thought of as similar to the recommendations consultants would give their clients at the end of consulting contracts. However, the similarity ends there. Typically, the consultant writes recommendations after their data analysis. In ASK, it is the participants, and not the consultants, who write the future-present scenarios. They are always written in the present tense, as if it has already happened. The FPS concept is based on pushing the limits of what is possible. Participants go as far as they can until the scenario may look unrealistic or lacking in commitment.

- Further, an individual participating in the process may have his or her own "favorite" KE and think it is more important than rest of the KEs. In such cases, he or she focuses more attention on that KE. Likewise, another may have a KE as "first among the equals" and may be keen to develop several FPSs for that one. Finally, such relative preferences may exist for KIFs as well. An individual may believe that "leadership is the most important thing we need to focus in this organization," while another may believe "unless we look at the organizational structure, we are not going anywhere with this process." Such preferences are likely and do not pose

(Continued next page)

any danger in biasing the FPS in any way. In a large sample, such individual preferences balance out.

- The consultant and facilitators should pay attention to the energy levels during the process. Writing FPSs almost always generates a great deal of enthusiasm and activity. If you find the process rather mechanical or lacking energy, you must confer with the client immediately to figure out what might have happened.
- Try to get visible support of the leadership at least in the initial stages of writing the FPSs. The physical presence of a senior manager and a statement from her, first, encouraging participants to be bold and creative in generating the FPS and, second, ensuring them of her support in the process in whatever ways she can will go a long way toward making the activity a success.

Chapter 8

Creating Consensus for Future-Present Scenarios

The consultant and the organizing group must carefully consider adding a second day to an ASK initiation project. In the case of Green Capital Bank, the large number of employees participating required extra time for processing the emerging data. Second, a pace that allows for a two-day event tends not to rush important decisions. In this instance, a single day to process the vast amount of data generated would clearly have been insufficient. Further, having overnight to reflect certainly facilitates the important concluding activities to follow the next day.

In the case of Green Capital Bank, the overnight reflection time strengthened the resolve of the group to complete the important steps begun the previous day. A certain kind of clarity about what knowledge sharing in Green Capital Bank is and should be obviously manifested itself on the morning of the second day. A new level of confidence and assertiveness was apparent in many members. The tentativeness of a few during the beginning of the previous day had all but disappeared, as they took charge and participated with enthusiasm. Even then, a few stragglers grabbed a last minute, "dalaying" cup of coffee as the knowledge ambassadors greeted participants at their tables.

After just a quick review of the previous day's process, the groups went back to work attentively. The groups, with the help of the knowledge ambassadors, checked the completed future-present scenarios from the previous day again against the criteria of commitment, groundedness, and inspiration. Then the groups visited other tables, commenting on each other's statements and the accomplishments they had made already. Eventually, based on learning from others, the groups wrote a revised set of future-present scenarios.

Writing future-present scenario statements was an exciting activity for the Green Capital Bank employees. Having an opportunity to participate in creating an innovative knowledge sharing process as a continuing reality was appealing to the employees, because it allowed them to express the sense of belonging they had felt for the organization and for the process itself. The experience proved very much like affirming McGregor's classic "Theory Y": given an opportunity, employees will work without supervision and will autonomously contribute to the good of the organization.

Arising from their commitment and enthusiasm, Green Capital Bank participants generated a large number of future-present scenarios. However, to act on all of them wouldn't be realistic, hence the need to prioritize them using a set of criteria. The criteria categorized the scenarios into a sequence of various action steps, including the importance or ideality of the future-present scenario, the actual presence of it already in the organization, and the desired speed of its implementation or realization in the organization.

Step 6: Consensually Validate and Rank the Future-Present Scenarios

The following three criteria served a balancing function, asking questions that make evaluating and exploring the potential of the statements possible. In the absence of the criteria, participants might, on the one hand, come up with action plans too radical or beyond the realm of possibility, or, on the other hand, merely mundane or trivial. By checking how much of a future-present scenario may be present currently, participants avoid a re-statement or rehashing of the status quo. Finally, by asking the timing question, "How soon does the participant want to see a given future-present scenario realized?" the decision makers get valuable data and feedback about the relative urgency employees attach to the various future-present scenarios.

Once participants wrote their future-present scenarios, they checked them again against the criteria listed in the previous section. Organizers then asked the various groups to look at other future-present scenarios and comment on each other's statements so that eventually they could write a revised final set of scenarios. Once completed, everyone in the group prioritized, ranked, or rated them using the following three questions.

- How much of an ideal is it? (How important is it?)

5	4	3	2	1
VERY MUCH				NOT MUCH

- How much of it may already be present?

5	4	3	2	1
VERY MUCH				NOT MUCH

- How soon do you want to see this happen?

IMMEDIATELY	SHORT TERM	LONG TERM
	(within 6 months)	(within two years)

Once the participants have finished prioritizing, organizers tabulate the scores. Participants now look for future-present scenarios with the maximum discrepancy between the IDEAL and the PRESENT, therefore needing IMMEDIATE implementation. At the end, the groups prioritize the propositions based on a set of criteria that are important to the organization.

Here is how the Green Capital Bank did it. A final re-writing and revising of the statements incorporated the comments and sentiments of other groups. As mentioned above, in the next step the groups at their tables rated the importance of each future-present scenario by listing the final statements on their own flip chart pages in the front of the ballroom, pasted to the wall. The top half of each flip chart contained a future-present scenario written in large-size letters. The bottom half of each flip chart listed the three questions for voting or rating (that is, how much of an ideal it is, how much of it is present now, and how soon would you like this to happen).

The knowledge ambassadors did a quick review of the posted charts to make sure they represented all knowledge enablers and at least one future-present scenario for each knowledge infrastructure factor.

The next step involved individual input. The knowledge ambassadors handed each member of their table a set of blue, green, and red round, bright-colored stickers, each color representing a question in the prioritizing flip chart (blue the ideal, green the current or present, and red the speed of realization). Participants expressed their preferences for each future-present scenario by sticking the colored dots next to their preferences. For example, for a particular future-present scenario, a staffer might stick a blue dot over the "5" rating (most ideal) whereas another staffer might stick a blue over the "3" rating for the same scenario. Similarly, an employee might place a green dot over the "1" rating (not present) while another might place a "2" for the same future-present scenario. By doing so, all bank employees in effect "voted" for the future-present scenarios they most fully supported or the ones they believed had the best chance for success.

Once the "sticking" was done, organizers tabulated the number of dots on each statement, deriving for each future-present scenario the difference between the ideal and the actual. Groups then looked for the future-present scenarios with the maximum discrepancy between the IDEAL and the PRESENT needing IMMEDIATE implementation. For example, assume 100 people participate in the "voting" process and that FPS #7 receives 65 ratings of 5 for "ideal" and the following for the "current" or "present": 50 for 1, 15 for 2, and 8 for 5. Clearly in this case a large number of people feel FPS #7 is highly desirable but not present currently, as evident by the large number of low 1 ratings it receives. After performing such calculations for each future-present scenario, organizers can transfer them to a Microsoft Excel table and perform all manner of calculations, depending on the quantitative inclinations or interests of the group. Most important is determining where the energy of the organization lies, as evidenced by which future-present scenarios receives proportionally high numbers of "ideal" 5 ratings and as well as noting which ones receive "current" 1 ratings and sizable "immediate" for the third question of implementation.

At the end of the Green Capital Bank's process, the organizers prioritized all the future-present scenarios through a set of criteria important to the organizational learning department and to the bank. The chief criterion was the time line. Future-present scenarios with high difference between the ideal and the current and high immediate implementation ratings were categorized for immediate follow-up and action. The future-present scenarios that received short term rating for the third item were categorized for closer examination with a larger audience. Finally, the long term future-present scenarios were categorized as strategically important and designated for further follow-up with all stakeholders, including customers and other players in the environment.

Chapter Summary

This chapter outlines the important step of validating the future-present scenarios [FPS]. In a way, this step is the culmination of the ASK process. The validation is very much like the voice of the people in the organization and represents their carefully thought-out assessment of where the organization is ready to go and the extent of their willingness to contribute to make each of the future scenarios a reality. For this reason, keeping the activity as participatory and representative as possible is critical. Participants in the validating should be those who can influence the future scenarios and at the same time are directly impacted by them. The capacity to influence and the willingness to be influenced are the two parallel processes underlying the validation stage.

Practitioner Focus Box

- Validating the future-present scenarios (FPSs) is one of the most intense and high-energy stages of the ASK process. A consultant might feel overwhelmed by the enthusiasm

(Continued next page)

and commitment of people during the validation activity. While you should do everything possible to keep the process in the high-energy mode, equally important is paying attention to the sequence of the validation process. If you notice that the participant group reveals a clear hierarchy, you may want to ensure that those in senior positions do not influence those less experienced or in a junior level. If a Vice President and manager look at the future-present scenarios posted on the walls together, and if the Vice President does his validation first, the manager is likely to be influenced by how the Vice President "votes." You can avoid such possibilities by thinking through the process in advance and coming up with a suggested sequence that avoids placing two individuals from the same unit or department at the same future-present scenarios at the same time. Alternatively, you can discuss this situation with the Vice President and suggest that he/she not observe others validating their propositions and wait to do his/her own validation until everyone else has exercised theirs.

- You should pay special attention to the visual aspects of the validation process. The room should be large with plenty of empty wall space for sticking up at least 40 flip charts with about 12 inches separating each future-present scenario. Participants must be able to move back and forth and across the hall/room freely without obstruction.
- Decide on a "traffic management plan" in advance. It is common to have participants congregating around the first few Future-Present-Scenarios or select few others while the space in front of several other Future-Present-Scenarios remains empty. You can make the process go smoothly by pre-assigning the first few Future-Present-Scenarios to each participant. This ensures that the group disperses equally in the beginning and that all scenarios receive a "fresh look" from some participants.

Chapter 9

From Paper to Action

As with most interventions, how an organization "closes" an event powerfully impacts what it achieves after the consultant is gone. The final and probably the most important step in the ASK process is first form action items and then forming teams to implement those action items. Many organizations do excellent work from Step 1 through 6 but struggle at step 7, forming an implementation team. To come up with exciting scenarios is, of course, important, but implementing them is another process all together, as pointed out most recently by well known corporate CEO, Larry Bossidy, and management guru, Ram Charan, in their book, *Execution: The Discipline of Getting Things Done* (2002). They define execution as closing the gap between promised results and delivered results. Bossidy and Charan correctly point out that, although getting things done (execution) does not sound as elegant as discussing strategy, vision, leadership development, or core competence, it is the vital "missing link between aspirations and results." Using stories of the "execution difference" being both won (EDS) and lost (Xerox and Lucent), they demonstrate that without execution, breakthrough thinking on managing change itself breaks down.

As Bossidy and Charan (2002) demonstrate, execution is a discipline of its own with a specific set of behaviors and techniques and (like ASK) is embedded in the culture of an organization. They show that many leaders create a culture of indecisiveness. Overcoming it requires generating honesty and connections among people, appreciating the organization's "social operating mechanisms" (meetings, reviews, etc.,) to create genuine dialogue, rewarding high achievers, and coaching those who are struggling. Bossidy and Charan (2002) assert that by using such approaches and considering every encounter as an opportunity to model true dialogue, a leader can set the cultural tone and impetus to move an organization from hesitation and too much analysis to execution.

Given the importance of execution, organization development practitioners and knowledge management consultants must make sure that the future-present scenarios [FPS] in the high priority list are indeed the ones for which a true desire for implementation exists. They may work with the client in setting up the implementation team and do periodic follow-up on how the process is working. A contract that includes an implementation phase is ideal in this context. In many cases, however, consultant involvement may end with step 6.

Step 7: Forming an Implementation Team

Green Capital Bank recognized that this step of forming an implementation team became the crossroads at which the project would become a success or no change would take place. So participants and the knowledge ambassadors took great care to verify that the propositions in the high priority list were the ones for which a true desire for implementation existed. Fortunately, the organizational learning department staff was not content with creating possibility propositions as an end. Being equally concerned about the bottom line, the participants, with active support of the organizational learning staff, generated action items from the possibility propositions that were specific to each business unit. Further, they identified several knowledge sharing initiatives and goals for the year in areas such as employee development, distance learning, leadership development, and project management.

Most participants volunteered to become the advocates or sponsors for action items and to take responsibility for the realization of the desired outcomes. They became sponsors if they had the power and responsibility for initiation and implementation of a given future-present scenario. Or, the members became advocates when, not having the formal power to make decisions, they did have the informal power to influence using their social capital and goodwill.

Later the knowledge ambassadors clearly felt significant investment in the process and as a result felt a sense of responsibility to maintain the momentum they had themselves generated and to make things happen in a timely manner. As a result, they divided up the future-present scenarios among themselves based on the advocacy/sponsorship dimension and their personal interest in them. Then they took the lead in setting up meetings with senior managers and sought their input, support, or permission for initiating and/or executing future-present scenarios.

The Ending of a New Beginning!

Green Capital Bank's appreciative sharing of knowledge event "ended" on a high note. Overall, the focus to reframe organizational reality in affirmative terms was so strong that one of the groups in the organizational learning department decided collectively that when they heard one another speak negatively about a situation they would challenge that person by asking him or her "If the situation you are talking about was just the way it should be, what would that look like? Now, how can we make that happen?"

Participants lingered after the session was over, talking about their action items and the work they had agreed to champion. More than a few participants commented, "This project was different. It was the best bank program I've ever attended." Participants could now see the possibilities at Green Capital Bank. They were enthusiastic and energized with the desire to continue working in the organizational learning department. Plus, they felt they had a stake in the organization.

With their action items in hand, they went to work!

Chapter Summary

This section highlights the importance of having a blueprint for implementation of the future-present scenarios. The chapter presents recent research on the topic of "execution" calling for particular alertness to all aspects of the prioritized future-present scenarios. An organization must be absolutely confident about the top future-present scenarios they pick for implementation. Once they make the decision, the process of execution unfolds with its own unique requirements and properties, as outlined in the chapter.

Practitioner Focus Box

- The process of implementing the validated and prioritized Future-Present Scenarios is one that will determine the eventual success or usefulness of the ASK. If the execution does not go far enough, a return to the status quo may be the outcome. Consultants and practitioners must also be aware that some resistance to change may be evident even when they frame the future-scenarios positively.

- In many situations, the consultant may not be part of the implementation step. Assuming the consultant knows this from the beginning, the consultant should take steps for a smooth transition of the ASK facilitation to the internal organizational development, human resources, or change department. A consultant's absence from the implementation process is ill advised if the client system is not properly prepared to engage in the complexities of execution.

- The implementation or execution stage may also provide data about the "soundness" of the ASK process used. If implementation becomes difficult or does not lead to the desired outcomes, the factors causing it probably were not detected during the earlier steps. Such contexts may provide valuable learning opportunities for both the consultant and the client system for future ASK project implementations.

Chapter 10

Emphasizing Learning Implications in the Knowledge Sharing Process

As with any project or program, through experiences and intelligent questions from the diverse participants at Green Capital Bank, everyone learned fascinating and valuable lessons. Highlighted below are the unexpected challenges faced by the management, staff, and consultant, their resolution, and the lessons learned.

Future-Present Scenarios as Road Maps

The various future-present scenario statements turned out to be a solid process through which Green Capital Bank embraced knowledge sharing. The process provided a road map to a specific location based on the tacit knowledge of the organizational members. Further, because of the participatory process used, the future-present scenarios brought out issues that needed addressing.

The Power of Reframing

The power of reframing in creating new knowledge sharing practices became immediately evident as a result of this project. The ASK process did not want to focus on deficits but at the same time did not deny the experiences people expressed. Instead of asking why the staff did not share knowledge, the question was reframed as, "What were the times you felt you shared knowledge with someone in your organization?" As the process of reframing continued throughout the ASK process, some members developed a natural habit of reframing that facilitated knowledge sharing.

Appreciation as a Facilitator for Innovation

When an organization appreciates and respects stakeholders for what they bring to the organizational arena and when it genuinely seeks and secures their participation, stakeholders generate innovative and powerful future-present scenarios. As recent research shows, appreciation helps people deal with the "resistance to change" issue present in most change efforts. Since no one blames others or fixes responsibility for the "wrongs done," participants are more willing to give ASK a chance to work.

The Importance of Getting to the Core

At the end of the one-day workshop before the ASK event, the knowledge ambassador facilitators were clearly having difficulty getting to the core of the stories. Because finding the true knowledge enablers was crucial to the success of ASK, they needed a way to go deeper than the surface reasons (such as, because my manager told me to, or because that's part of my job, or I needed a job).

Eliciting deep conversation takes both time and skill. With only limited time available during the interviews, the knowledge ambassadors had to make the best use of their time to draw out meaningful responses from the interviewees. To help the knowledge ambassadors conduct good interviews and elicit deep conversation in a group setting, they were trained in small-group facilitation methods, including techniques for asking questions without intimidating; getting into greater depth of conversation successively, one step at a time, without rushing, despite the lack of time; being mindful to affirm interviewees or group members for what they share; not judging the quality of responses unnecessarily; and ending the process by making sure that the interviewees or group members shared what they wanted to share and held nothing back. Following this strategy helped get to the core of the knowledge sharing goal.

The Important Role of the Knowledge Ambassadors

The ASK process assigns a key role for the knowledge ambassadors in facilitating change through knowledge sharing. They, instead of the consultant, drive the process after the intervention. After all, they are Green Capital Bank employees who have a much better sense of the organization than the consultant and naturally have a significant stake in the success and survival of their organization. Finally, they have the flexibility and possess the subject knowledge of their specific operational areas, thereby enabling them to coach colleagues for follow-up work on the future-present scenarios.

Later, at the ASK event, the knowledge ambassadors needed to keep participants grounded in concrete and specific action mode rather than in the abstract and the general. Since part of the success of the ASK project depends upon the ability of the participants to visualize their future-present scenarios, the more real the future-present scenarios seem, the more the participants feel they have a stake in realizing them, much the way someone works toward realizing a dream she wants "so badly she can taste it." Because future-present scenarios tend to be abstract, knowledge ambassadors must continuously remind the participants to be concrete and to think in terms of the sensory. To aid the process, they learned to ask variations of two key facilitative questions: "When you mentally put yourself in that situation, what does it look like? What do you hear?" or, "If the situation were to change in a way you would like, what would that look like?"

Grounding Future-Present Scenarios

As mentioned in the previous chapter, vital to success is helping the participants visualize a concrete reality based on a full realization of the future-present scenarios [FPS]. If a given FPS comes true, do the stakeholders really want to engage in that mode? For example, if the FPS for regular Friday late-afternoon meetings comes true, will the members really like that after a while? Some may feel "I don't want to give up my Friday afternoon." Perhaps what was really important was having a regular forum to communicate openly. Hence, Mondays would have been just as good as Fridays. In other words, organizations must pay special attention to each element of the future-present scenarios, whether, as in this example, face-to-face meetings, the day of meetings (Monday or Friday), the time of meetings (low energy time versus high-energy time), the composition of participants (Who will attend? Will the boss be there?), the focus of meetings (content of discussion), and the regularity (daily, weekly, or monthly?).

An important aspect is that a future-present scenario may sound exciting, appealing, or radical, yet it may not be based on an accurate identification of knowledge enablers or a realistic assessment of their interaction with knowledge infrastructure factors. In other words, one must distinguish between *social desirability* and *social feasibility*. The former is a strong motivator and may subtly encourage participants to pick action items that look good or may win the approval of top management. The latter, social feasibility, is more realistic and often less attractive and hence may not gather much momentum in large settings such as the ones described in the Green Capital Bank example.

Organizers must steer participants to future-present scenarios high on social feasibility rather than on social desirability, partly by constructing the FPS checklist and the commitment, inspiration, and groundedness model described in Chapter 7. An equally sound indicator for the authenticity of a future-present scenario is the subjective intuition that the participants, the knowledge ambassadors, or the key client contacts may have about it. This is an area where consultants typically have limited knowledge because they have not been part of the organizational system long enough. However, consultants may make-up for this, first, by intentionally encouraging or coaching the knowledge ambassadors and participants to trust their intuitions and, second, by periodically reaffirming that doing so does not negate the more rigorous process undertaken earlier to write the future-present scenarios.

Closing the Event but Not the Process

By design, the ASK project does not have a well-defined ending, because knowledge sharing never ends. The ASK project is more like the beginning of a new process, though the event itself ends. Keeping this lesson in mind is crucial to success: management and/

or participants believe they have become a knowledge sharing entity simply by virtue of the project's completion. On the contrary, an organization must gain commitment for follow-up work to implement the future-present scenarios.

The Green Capital Bank employees felt differently about ASK in comparison to other organizational activities they had done. Some contrasted it to an event the previous year in which everyone also came together; however, they reported that the earlier activity did not have the same power or generate the same enthusiasm as the ASK process did. They felt that the ASK process allowed them to use "real" data from "real life" work experiences with plenty of specificity. In addition, they liked not blaming or fixing responsibilities for what went wrong, but focusing on what went right.

Several of the attendees highlighted the different climate of this session. The "free-floating" climate of affirming one another is something unique to ASK and especially unique to their experience.

Finally, they reported that they really learned and felt that everyone had something to contribute to the knowledge sharing process. Whether they were a Vice President or data processing staffer, they were listened to. It felt good.

Chapter 11

Reflections

The ASK project concluded with the successful attainment of Green Capital Bank's original goal and further far-reaching results. The consultant's goal was to help them assess a range of knowledge management programs as well as assist them in adopting a single knowledge sharing methodology that integrated the different knowledge management tools across their business units. He achieved both results through the appreciative sharing approach, as evidenced by the self-report of the participants.

Whether the organization be a corporation, nonprofit, government agency, or community of practice within a larger organization, all groups reap significant benefits from appreciative knowledge sharing. ASK is both a non-threatening and accepting approach that makes people realize that what they do *does* make a difference. The simplicity of ASK is its power. Organizations can use ASK for a variety of issues relating to knowledge management. For example, implementing the future-present scenarios might require some form of restructuring of the organization. Or, it might necessitate creating a team-based structure or flattening of hierarchies. At this stage, ASK translates into traditional organizational development or change management work in which the original Appreciative Inquiry [AI] approach might be re-applicable.

The simplicity of ASK does not mask the need to go through all the steps as listed below.

Step 1: Set the stage. Present the appreciative knowledge sharing paradigm, and negotiate top management commitment and support.

Step 2: Through paired interviews, elicit positive stories of successful knowledge sharing behaviors already occurring.

Step 3: Identify knowledge enablers [KE].

Step 4: Analyze the data using knowledge infrastructure factors.

Step 5: Construct Future-Present Scenarios [FPS].

Step 6: Consensually validate and rank Future-Present-Scenarios

Step 7: Form an implementation team. Then execute!

Rather than starting (and sometimes not finishing) a knowledge management project that merely becomes one more initiative, one more change for employees to get used to, ASK leads to an organic, self-perpetuating culture that—as designed by members of their own organization—is custom-made for a business. The intrinsic rewards are the knowledge and the sharing of it that we as humans strongly desire. Following the above steps makes your organization more successful by establishing, encouraging, and solidifying a sense of excellence through knowledge sharing, and thereby creates value for all stakeholders. In an era where knowledge is power and intellectual capital is the most strategic and competitive resource base of organizations, investing and engaging in this simple but powerful method should be one of the most worthwhile investments an organization can make for long-term growth and innovation.

Several thoughts stayed with me long after the ASK project ended with Green Capital Bank. Foremost is the realization that the most powerful interventions in an organization may also be the simplest. The term "simple" does not, however, mean lack of depth or understanding. On the contrary, the ASK approach shows a sophisticated understanding of knowledge sharing in organizations. Margaret Wheatley and Myron Kellner-Rogers (1999) devoted a book-length study to this theme in *A Simpler Way*. "There is a simpler way to organize human endeavor," they write. "It requires a new way of being in the world. It requires being in the world without fear. Being in the world with play and creativity. Seeking after what's possible. Being willing to learn and to be surprised." Looking back at the Green Capital Bank experience and others in which I used ASK, I can fully validate their statement. At the same time, I also wonder how to respond constructively and not critically to those decision makers in organizations who invest significant material as well as human and financial resources to create knowledge management architecture rooted deeply in the modernist world-view of predictability and uncertainly reduction. One of the challenges for me as a practitioner interested in promoting the ASK method is to be conscious and appreciative of such paradoxes of organizational life. I am also aware that ASK is not a panacea for all knowledge management problems, that in certain situations ASK is not the most appropriate approach.

Yet, in summary, if people are valued for whatever contributions they make, and if the organizational architecture supports what enables knowledge sharing, the stakeholders will be genuinely interested in contributing to the success and growth of their organization.

Closing with a Re-emphasis on the Social Construction of ASK

This Focus Book begins by discussing the foundations of the ASK process, as embedded in the philosophical tenets of social constructionism. Revisiting these tenets is important at this concluding stage as well. In *An Invitation to Social Construction*, Kenneth Gergen (1999) asks readers to go beyond deconstruction to a generative action mind-set. The possibility that facts and beliefs can be deconstructed must not discourage imaginative theory building around knowledge creation and sharing. Similarly, Karl Weick (1989; 1999) argues that theory construction is a form of disciplined imagination and reflexivity. After all, many innovations in organizations emerge from the power of inspiring ideas rather than from concrete empirical support. This is especially true in the case of change processes that include attention to knowledge sharing and inclusion.

Kenneth Gergen posits that the socially constructed nature of knowledge management allows practitioners to be bold and evocative about the nature and type of new knowledge creation initiatives. He invites us to go beyond the limited notions of individual monologs and embrace transformative dialogues, "In a world in which the globalizing process brings opposing realties into increasingly sharp conflict, new resources for communication seem essential" (1999, p. 164). Such knowledge sharing conversations eventually help us create more innovations in organizations and move them from "good to great." Jim Collins (2001) frames such a question in researching how organizations can go from "good to great." Collins asks, *"Why Some Companies Make the Leap and Others Don't?"* in his book of the same title. After reading and coding 6,000 articles and generating more than 2,000 pages of interview transcripts, Collins finds that making the transition from good to great doesn't require a high-profile CEO, the latest technology, or even a fine-tuned business strategy. At the heart of great companies is a corporate culture that rigorously finds and promotes disciplined people to think and act in a disciplined manner. Though Collins doesn't call it so, knowledge sharing with an appreciative mindset is a key ingredient of that discipline.

Consultants Eric Schiffer and Robert Nelson (2003) use the concept of "emotionally charged learning" that they claim holds the key to the secrets to competitive advantages for the knowledge-based economy. "How does an OK company become an excellent company?" they ask. To find out they collected data on what the excellent companies do and conclude that they are leveraging effective knowledge capital growth, yet another process closely related to ASK.

Irrespective of the terms used, the latest research and practice suggest the need to be intentional, proactive, or generative about knowledge creation and sharing. The ASK process is one that focuses on the process aspect of knowledge sharing, that is, "How can we help organizations do better what they already do well by leveraging the knowledge enablers and knowledge infrastructure factors?" The result must be a solid appreciative sharing of knowledge process [ASK] for the critical knowledge sharing to occur in organizations.

References

Argyris, C. (1993). *Knowledge for action: A guide to overcoming barriers to organizational change*. San Francisco, CA: Jossey-Bass.

Argyris, C. (1990). *Overcoming Organizational Defenses*. Boston: Allyn and Bacon.

Berger, P., & Luckman, T. (1966). *The social construction of reality*. New York: Anchor Books.

Bossidy, l., & Charan, R., (2002). *Execution: The Discipline of Getting Things Done*. New York: Crown Business.

Bourdieu, B. P., & Wacquant, L.P. (1992). *An invitation to reflexive sociology*. Chicago: University of Chicago Press.

Collins, J., (2001). *Good to Great: Why Some Companies Make the Leap and Others Don't*. New York: HarperCollins.

Cooperrider, D., Whitney, D., & Stavros, J. (2003). *Appreciative Inquiry: The Handbook*. Bedford Heights, OH: Lake Shore Publishers.

Cooperrider, D., & Srivastva, S. (1987). Appreciative Inquiry in organizational life. *Research in Organizational Change and Development, 1*, pp. 129-169.

Ehin, C. (2000). *Unleashing Intellectual Capital*. Boston: Butterworth-Heinemann

Gergen, K. J., & Gergen, M. (Eds.). (2003). *Social Construction: A Reader*. Thousand Oaks, CA: Sage.

Gergen, K. J. (1999). *An Invitation to Social Construction*. Thousand Oaks, CA: Sage.

Herzberg, F., Mausner, B., & Snyderman, B. B. (1959). *The Motivation to Work*. New York: John Wiley & Sons.

Kierein, N., & Gold, M. (2000). Pygmalion in work organizations: A meta-analysis. *Journal of Organizational Behavior*, 21 (8), 913 – 924.

Lewin, K. (1947). Group Decision and Social Change. In T. Newcomb & E. L. Hartley (Eds.). *Readings in Social Psychology* (pp. 340-344). New York: Holt & Co.

Lewin, K. (1951/1997). *Field Theory in Social Science*. American Psychological Association, Washington, DC.

Lyotard, J.F. (1984). *The Postmodern Condition: A report on knowledge* (B. Massouri, Trans.). Minneapolis: University of Minnesota Press.

Lyotard, J. F. (1988). *The Inhuman: Reflections on Time* (G. Bennington & R. Bowlby, Trans.). Cambridge, MA: Polity, 1988.

Maslow, A. (1954). *Motivation and Personality*. New York: Harper and Row.

McGregor D. (1960). *The Human Side of Enterprise*. New York: McGraw Hill.

Murphy, D., Campbell, C., & Garavan, T. (1999). The Pygmalion effect reconsidered: its implications for education, training and workplace learning. *Journal of European Industrial Training*, 23 (4/5), 238 – 249.

Polyani, M. (1967). *The Tacit Dimension*, Garden City, NY: Anchor Books.

Putnam, R. (2001). *Bowling Alone: The Collapse and Revival of American Community*. New York: Touchstone Books.

Reynolds, D. (2002). The good, the bad, and the ugly of incorporating "my fair lady" in the workplace. *S.A.M. Advanced Management Journal*. 67 (3), 4-11.

Rogers, C. (1980/1995). *A Way of Being*. Boston: Houghton Mifflin.

Rogers, C. (1961/1995). *On Becoming a Person*. Boston: Houghton Mifflin.

Rowe, G., & O'Brien, J. (2002). The role of Golem, Pygmalion, and Galatea effects on opportunistic behavior in the classroom. *Journal of Management Education*, 26 (6), 612-629.

Seligman, M. (1990). *Learned Optimism*. New York: Knopf.

Seligman, M., Maier, S., & Geer, J. (1968). The alleviation of learned helplessness in dogs. *Journal of Abnormal Psychology*, 73, 256-262.

Schiffer, E., & Nelson, B. (2003). *Emotionally Charged Learning: Secrets to Competitive Advantages for the Second Half of the Knowledge/Entertainment-Based Economy*. New York: Literary Press.

Schiff, M. (1992). Social capital, labor mobility, and welfare: The impact of uniting states. *Rationality and Society*, 4, 157-175.

Weick, K. (1989). Theory Construction as Disciplined Imagination. *Academy of Management Review*, 14 (4), 516-532.

Weick, K. (1999). Theory Construction as Disciplined Reflexivity: Tradeoffs in the 90s. *Academy of Management Review*, 24 (4), 797- 807.

Wheatley, M., & Kellner-Rogers, M. (1999). *A Simpler Way*. San Francisco: Berrett-Koehler.

Endnotes

[1] Green Capital Bank is the fictitious name of the bank that the consultant worked with and wishes to remain anonymous.

[2] Steve Fuller of University of Warwick thinks this is an instance of "catachresis," that is, the strategic misuse of words.

[3] http://appreciativeinquiry.cwru.edu is by far the most comprehensive source of information about Appreciative Inquiry. The Department of Organizational Behavior at Case Western Reserve University, Cleveland, Ohio, U.S.A., where the approach originated, maintains the site.

[4] To learn more about Kenneth Gergen's exhaustive work on social constructionism and The Taos Institute that intentionally uses the philosophy in its work, see www.taosinstitute.net. Also see Gergen, Kenneth and Mary Gergen. (2004). Editors. *Social Construction: A Reader*. Sage, and Gergen, Kenneth and Mary Gergen (2004). *Social Construction: Entering the Dialogue*. The Taos Institute Press.

Other useful sources are: (1) Anderson, Harlene. (1997). *Conversation, language, and possibilities: A postmodern approach to therapy*. New York: Basic Books and (2) Freedman, Jill., and Combs, Gene. (1996). *Narrative Therapy: The Social Construction of Preferred Realities*. New York: W.W. Norton.

[5] The term 'hermeneutics' comes from the classical Greek verb *hermeneuein, to interpret*. During the 17th century, hermeneutic study emerged as a discipline devoted to establishing guidelines for the proper interpretation of Biblical scripture. Since then, hermeneutics has evolved into a form of inquiry primarily concerned with the processes by which human beings interpret or discover the meaning of human action. According to hermeneutical philosophy, language is the medium of all human experience. "Language allows humans to dwell in the house of being .

. . Language is the fundamental mode of operation of our being-in- the- world and an all-embracing form of the constitution of the world" (Gadamer, 1977, p 3). The human world is linguistically pre-constituted. We inherit language in the 'social uterus'. In other words, language precedes us in the world. Human understanding takes place within an emerging linguistic framework evolved over time in terms of historically conditioned concerns and practices.

Some of the important writings in hermeneutics are: 1) Gadamer, Hans Georg. (1977). *Philosophical Hermeneutics*. Berkeley, CA: University of California Press. 2) Ricoeur, P (1981). *Hermeneutics and the Human Sciences*. (Trans. J.B. Thompson). Cambridge: Cambridge University Press. 3) Wittgenstein, L. (1963) *Philosophical investigations*. (G. Anscombe, trans.) New York: Macmillan. For an example of using hermeneutics in organizational analysis, see Thatchenkery, Tojo (2001). Mining for meaning: Reading organizations using hermeneutic philosophy. In Westwood, R.I., & Linstead, S. A. (Editors) *The Language of Organization*. London: Sage, pp.112-131

[6] In simple terms, self-referentiality implies that all rules refer to other rules and have validity only in the context of such a network of inter-dependent relationships. Self-referential also relates to the ways in which postmodern narrative often self-consciously comments upon itself during the writing, drawing the reader's attention to writing as a construct.

[7] A term introduced by Seligman (1991) to explain why people look at the same reality in entirely different ways. While some see despair, others may see hope depending on their explanatory style.

[8] See James E. Maddux, Stopping the "Madness": Positive Psychology and the Deconstruction of Illness Ideology and the *DSM* in *Handbook of Positive Psychology*, edited by C. R. Snyder and Shane J. Lopez, NY: Oxford University Press, pp. 13-25.

[9] The Mirrian Webster's dictionary defines the verb "to appreciate" in the following way.
-To grasp the nature, worth, quality, and or significance of
-To judge with heightened perception of understanding
-To increase the value of
Thus, in appreciation, there is a process of selectivity and judgment. The perceiver is choosing to look at some stimuli intently and in the process see them more fully.

[10] Steve Denning has consistently used the "story telling" approach in knowledge management. See Denning, Steve (2004), *Squirrel Inc. A fable of leadership through storytelling*. San Francisco: Jossey-Bass, and Denning, Steve (2000), *The Springboard: How Storytelling Ignites Action in Knowledge-Era Organizations*, Boston: Butterworth-Heinemann for a good introduction to the approach.

[11] The Pygmalion effect or self-fulfilling prophecy, long recognized by teachers, physicians, and behavioral scientists, states that one's expectations shape another person's behavior. Numerous case studies and research exist to demonstrate the importance of managerial expectations to individual and group performance. If managers believe that employees will perform poorly, they cannot hide their low expectations. Further, managers' beliefs about themselves influence how they view and treat their employees. Superior managers have high expectations of their subordinates partly because they have better self-esteem and belief in their own abilities.

[12] See the book *Identity, Learning, and Decision Making in Changing Organizations* by Charles Schwenk, Westport, CT: Quorum, 2002, for a good contextual understanding of decision making and knowledge sharing. A number of good books have been written over the years about obstacles to effective decision making in organizations and how to overcome them: *Decision Making* by Janis and Mann (1977), *Decision Traps* by Russo and Shoemaker (1989), and *Why Decisions Fail* by Nutt (2002). Other

good sources are: The role of intuition in strategic decision making by Naresh Khatri and Alvin Ng, *Human Relations*, 2000, 53, 1, 57 - 87; and *Managerial Decision Making - Part 2: The Newer Techniques*, Kharbanda, O. P., Stallworthy, E. A. Management Decision, 1990, 28, 4, 29 -36.

[13] John Seely Brown and Paul Duguid introduced the term "Communities of Practice" in their paper "Organizational Learning and Communities of Practice: Toward A Unified View of Working, Learning and Innovation." Management Science, February 1991. See *Communities of Practice: Learning, Meaning, and Identity* by Etienne Wenger, Cambridge University Press, New York, 1998 for a good treatment on CoP and developments since 1991.

[14] See *Cultivating Communities of Practice* by Etienne Wenger, Richard McDermott, William M. Snyder Harvard Business School Press, 2002, and *Leveraging Communities of Practice for Strategic Advantage* by Hubert Saint-Onge, Debra Wallace Butterworth-Heinemann, 2003, for a compilation of evidences supporting CoP and knowledge sharing.

About the Author

Tojo Thatchenkery (Ph.D. in Organizational Behavior, Weatherhead School of Management, Case Western Reserve University) is a professor of organizational learning & knowledge management at George Mason University, Fairfax, Virginia, U.S.A. He has over twenty years of experience in teaching at various MBA, Public Policy, Organizational Development, and executive programs in the United States, Europe, Australia, and Asia. Professor Thatchenkery founded the Organizational Learning Laboratory at the George W. Johnson Learning Center at George Mason University and served as its director from 1995 to 2000.

Professor Thatchenkery has extensive consulting experience with knowledge management, organization design, change management, and various aspects of human resources management. Past clients include the IBM, Fannie Mae, Booz/Allen/Hamilton, Lucent Technologies, General Mills, British Petroleum, the International Monetary Fund, the World Bank, United States Department of Agriculture, and the Environmental Protection Agency. He has also developed subject matter expertise in helping Asian Americans and other minority groups leverage their human and social capital for organizational mobility and has worked with several Fortune 100 companies and federal agencies on this issue.

Professor Thatchenkery is on the editorial board of the *Journal of Applied Behavioral Sciences* and the *Journal of Organizational Change Management*. He is also the book review editor for the *Journal of Organizational Change Management*. Professor Thatchenkery has over 30 refereed publications on topics such as postmodern management, organizational learning, change management, knowledge management, and organizational diversity. His current research interests include Information Communication Technology (ICT) and economic development of South East and South Asian countries, social capital and organizational mobility of Asian Americans, appreciative inquiry and hermeneutics as methodologies for understanding organizational change, and facilitative strategies for knowledge management.

CPSIA information can be obtained at www.ICGtesting.com
Printed in the USA
BVOW07s1909300713

327372BV00002B/105/P